Why God Planted
a Vineyard

Why God Planted a Vineyard

Prophetic Insights for Today's Church

Martin Richards

New Wine Press

New Wine Ministries
PO Box 17
Chichester
West Sussex
United Kingdom
PO19 2AW

ISBN 1–903725–84–4

Typeset by CRB Associates, Reepham, Norfolk
Cover design by CCD, www.ccdgroup.co.uk
Printed in Malta

Dedication

To my lovely wife Janice, without whose tireless support and encouragement, nothing would have ever been written.

Contents

What Others Are Saying About This Book...

"Martin's excellent book takes a foundational truth, God's vine and vineyard, and illuminates it with the light of personal experience and revelation. This book is a must for those wishing to go deeper into an understanding of our need, as individuals and as God's people, to abide in Christ the vine. Read it and be blessed!"

John Noble
Author, Chairman of Charismata –
the National Charismatic Leaders Conference

"Martin's gifting in capturing and riding the wave of God's presence is felt in his writing and his playing. Jump in and experience God!"

Steve Witt
Pastor, Metro Church South, Ohio, USA

"Martin Richards is a prophetic leader of our time who is being given a deeper understanding of God's season and purpose for His Church today. This book, whilst giving an accurate and timely prophetic insight into God's revealed will for today's Church, incorporates an understanding of the significance and symbolism of vineyard cultivation and wine production together with a prophetic message to His people in this end-time." *Ray Djan*
Leader, True Vine International Apostolic Resource Ministry

"Martin Richards is a founding member of Follys End Church and manifests the delicate balance of bringing authentic prophecy in a spirit of love and grace. He has had a tremendous impact on our church this year by bringing significant words from the Lord which have proven true, even in extremely unexpected ways! This book is a reflection of Martin's heart: 'Lord, that You would give us the spirit of wisdom and revelation that we may know You better.' I wholeheartedly recommend it to anyone who longs for the deeper things of the Lord and to find the 'hidden treasures' of knowledge and wisdom."   **Chris Roe**

Pastor, Follys End Church, Croydon

Introduction

Sometimes the revelation of God comes in an instant, forcing an instantaneous paradigm shift in our thinking. God has spoken to us and we feel satiated and elated, and rightly so. We are familiar with this as Christians and place upon it a description of "prophecy". If we were careless, this kind of instant word could easily become our expected and sole experience of how God speaks to us. But at other times, God's revelation can take an age: at first whetting our appetite with an interest, and then following with the gradual illumination of a growing light, opening unsought-after avenues of fascination, developing whole new understandings of Him and His ways, and leaving us in awe at the wonderful, loving care by which He guides and teaches us.

The revelation in this book falls easily into the second category. Though the pace of the revelation has increased sharply in latter years, its roots go back almost thirty years to a time when the author did not even know the God who was busy sowing His seed for a later harvest. It all began with a simple vision to plant a vineyard in the United Kingdom and drink the wine from it! The momentous event of meeting that loving God was still five years away, and though that encounter brought life to the author, it brought death to the vision. Not a cruel, untimely death, more of a fading away to obscurity in favour of far better dreams and visions, but nevertheless, a complete death. In fact, a darkness so impenetrable, yet so beautifully designed by God as to give the perfect conditions for germination. Germination, of course, requires darkness, but once the process has begun, light must come quickly for growth to be sustained.

The darkness surrounding the seed of this hidden vision lasted eleven years, but once the germination burst through into light there was no stopping it. Sometimes I wonder if it will ever end, and yet there is always a time for completion, a time to harvest what has been sown.

Chapter 1
Of God, Creation and Communication

At the bottom of my garden there is a plaque on the wall with an old poem on it. You may have come across it.

The kiss of the sun for pardon
The song of the birds for mirth
You are nearer God's heart in a garden
Than anywhere else on earth.

Before I became a Christian I used to think it was a bit cheesy. It reminded me of old fashioned birthday cards with rather mundane little verses on them. But increasingly, as I get to know more of the great God of creation, I see that it speaks a beautiful truth.

God communicates with us in many different ways and as with most parents, it is much easier for us to see what our Father is really like by looking at what He does. For us that means looking at His creation. He's a bit of a gardener you know. He created an entire world, planted it and landscaped it, even an entire universe! He planted a garden, Eden, for His special creation to live in. And He planted a vineyard which He tends and cares for. Jesus got close to His Father in a garden, Gethsemane, and made His first resurrected appearance in a garden. He likes giving life to things that grow and being around them and if we will look, we will see His characteristic hand and wisdom in them.

Don't let's fall into the trap sprung in the Garden of Eden by the serpent and think there is a better, more rational, cerebral or intellectual wisdom higher than God's. God is quite clear He has the wisdom, not us.

> " 'I will destroy the wisdom of the wise,
> And bring to nothing the understanding of the prudent.'
>
> Where is the wise? Where is the scribe? Where is the disputer of this age? Has not God made foolish the wisdom of this world?"
> (1 Corinthians 1:19–20)

I once worked with a man, a scientist and atheist, who asked me as a bit of a calligrapher, to write out something he found fascinating:

> If the human mind was so simple that we could understand it
> We would be so simple that we would not be able to.

His scientific mind found this amusing and thought provoking, but being in love with Jesus, I instantly found myself adapting it to describe man's relationship with God.

> If God was so simple that we could understand Him
> We would be God and He would not!

God is much bigger than you and I and He persists in talking to us through all of His creation, bypassing our wonderful cognitive powers and making a mockery of the wisdom of this world.

> "For since the creation of the world His invisible attributes are clearly seen, being understood by the things that are made, even His eternal power and Godhead."
> (Romans 1:20)

This means that everything that you and I can see of creation: mountains, rivers, glaciers, the stars, the sun and the moon, rain, trees, flowers, all vegetation, all of the animal kingdom, including all beasts, fishes, birds, insects and, of course, His highest creation man, will reveal God to us. In other words, if you ever want to know what He is like, take a look at what He made and you will see His character stamped all over it. You will begin to understand God's character and the way He works and thinks.

It's not a complicated process. In fact we humans understand it very well, though we may not always be aware of it. I'm a musician, a jazz saxophone player, and I listen to lots of other sax players. If you play me a CD of the famous players, I can usually tell you who it is because the music will have their characteristics indelibly printed in it. All musicians have certain phrases they like to play and create a particular sound from their instrument. They express themselves uniquely and whether we are musicians or not, we all do the same. The style of the emails you send, the clothes you choose, the music you listen to, your likes and dislikes, your actions, reactions and the way you speak; everything you do reveals your invisible attributes.

Let's put it another way. A friend of mine once went to the Natural History Museum in London. He was fascinated by the neatly labelled rows of old bones, and because of the progressive way they had been laid out, the conclusion the scientists had drawn that the bones therefore "proved" the theory of evolution: this joint developed into this more complex one, and then to this sophisticated one ten million years later, and so on. My friend's spirit was troubled because he knew that God's Word says that He created all the animals, not that they evolved. Yet he could see the scientific and human logic at work. It seemed quite plausible that a bone in one creature should evolve into a slightly different shape and use in another animal. So he asked God, "What's the answer?" and the Lord answered him immediately. "It's simple," He replied, "they all had the same designer, Me."

God's original idea in the Garden of Eden with Adam and Eve

was that He would gradually teach them from His own wisdom as they walked obediently past the Tree of the Knowledge of Good and Evil each day. He wanted to teach them through intimate relationship. I have no doubt that He would have liked to pass on this wisdom using the creation around them to illustrate His points. I see no reason in Scripture to suggest that God has changed His mind.

I sometimes wonder what it was like being Adam and Eve in the garden before the fall. I can imagine them asking the Lord all kinds of interesting questions just before nightfall. My children always asked me the meaty questions just as I was about to say, "Goodnight" and put the lights out. I wonder if that's a legacy from that time in the garden! Did Adam and Eve store up questions from the day to ask God as He walked in the garden in the cool of the evening before He put the big light of the sun out?

"Oh Father, we've been looking at Your trees and we've noticed that they all grow upwards. Why don't they grow out to the side or start out going up and then go down? Why is it always straight up?" And I can hear the answer. "I wondered when you would ask that! And I'm glad you have. You see, all living things need the light to grow. Before I made the sun they took energy from My light, but now that I have made the sun and given the dominion of the world to you, they grow towards the light of the sun I have made. The sunlight gives them energy to grow and become strong so they always reach straight up towards it. All My plants seek out the light and grow towards it because they 'know' that the light is good for them and that they are resourced and energised by it. Now understand something of great importance for you. I am your light and just like the plants with the sun, I will give you everything you need to grow strong and healthy, but you must keep reaching out to Me just like the trees and plants. Similarly, if the trees tried to grow away from the light, they would not grow strong and tall in the way I have intended, but would be weak and ragged and would wither away to dust. The same is true for you."

What an awesome experience it must have been in Eden! The very name means "pleasure" and it was the environment God Himself planted for man to dwell in. Have you ever realised that God got His hands dirty for us! He could just have said, "Now let there be a beautiful garden," and it would have happened just as when He made the heavens and the earth, the seas, the sun, moon and stars, and the animals and vegetation. But He didn't. He wanted to put His special, personal touch on the garden to make sure it was just right for us. Then He got His hands mucky again when He made Adam and later Eve. The word in Genesis 2:7, *yawtsar*, which we translate as "made" or "formed", carries the meaning of "sculpting" or "creating" in the same way as a potter would form a lump of clay. God did not just say, "Let there be man" and there was Adam! He came down to the earth, took the clay in His hands and modelled him in His own image! What an amazing story. Maybe He even had Jesus stand by the lump of clay and be the actual model!

The garden was arranged especially for man to live in and it wasn't a small allotment! It was huge! It was in the region that today we know as the country of Iraq. God even irrigated the garden by putting an extensive watering system in it that was so big it fed four rivers including the Tigris and the Euphrates. Who knows what this river was or where its source was? Perhaps it was the river of goodness and wholeness that flows from the presence of God that is referred to in Ezekiel and Revelation. We don't know and Scripture doesn't tell us, but what we do know is that it's not there now and that most of that region is desert and largely waterless. Since the fall of man and his subsequent expulsion from Eden, what had been a joy to keep and cultivate has now become toil and struggle, full of thorns and thistles, hard rock, sand and dust.

Sadly, and particularly in Western culture, we are losing touch with God's environment and fabricating our own. I don't think we're making a very good job of it. More than 80% of Americans live in big cities and Europe is following the same trend. One

reason we struggle to meet environmental targets is that we are
so divorced from the real environment!

I find it immensely sad when even teenage children have said to
me that they have never seen a real cow or a field of wheat or the
sea, because they live in a city and have never been out of it. I
long to get out of the city and just see the sky. I was brought up
on the edge of the Fen country in East Anglia, where I would
often stand in awe at the majestic canopy of the sky all around and
above; ever changing and displaying the greatest lighting shows
on earth. Now, living in the city, some days all I see is a narrow
strip of sky directly overhead, but I'm usually too distracted by
what's happening at ground level to notice even that. At night
the stars sing of the reality and the glory of God, but the city cuts
them out for the necessity of street lighting. Perhaps our
manifestation of what a city is, is more satanically-inspired than
God-inspired, after all, he envied the beauty of the stars and
wanted to be above them.

> *"I will exalt my throne above the stars of God."*
>
> (Isaiah 14:13)

So much is lost to us in our cities that God gave for our uplifting
and to draw us closer to Him. Not that cities are bad, we will all
live in one some day, a new Jerusalem built for us by God
Himself, but that city will not need the revealing trappings of
creation because it will be lit by the light of the Creator Himself.
But on earth, God loves to speak through His creation, inspiring
men with thoughts bigger than themselves and encouraging them
to consider eternity and God.

Chapter 2
A Vision Birthed

Many years before I became a Christian I developed an interest in the making of English Country wines. You can make wine from virtually anything you like, and once you understand the principles, it's quite easy to get started. Weird and wonderful concoctions were soon bubbling merrily away in our utility room, from elderberry to parsnip, dandelion to tea, orange to rice. But I'm afraid the taste was not very good. In fact we soon got fed up with our efforts and left what we had bottled in a cellar under the front steps. Only when we came to do some major building works on the house did we have to decide whether to drink the wine or throw it away. And then, what a surprise! – the wine had somehow changed its flavour over two or three years doing nothing and become very pleasant.

This encouragement soon made us start again after the building work, and I began to search for something I could brew that would be quick and give us something to drink whilst the precious country wines were maturing. I suppose it was something of a Homer Simpson "doh" moment when I realised that the answer was to grow my own grapes. Not that Homer had been "born" then and of course, growing your own grapes is not something you do overnight.

To begin with, the question had to be answered, could you

grow the right kind of grapes in England? The answer came in one of those strange coincidences that I now tend to call God-incidences! Just as I began to think about my idea, a series of articles appeared in a national newspaper charting the growth of English vine growing and wine making.

The Romans had brought vines here from mainland Europe and grown them successfully nearly two thousand years ago – an idea that was adopted and developed by the many monasteries that sprung up over the centuries. Though most of these vineyards were destroyed during the reign of Henry VIII, grape growing was widely established in southern Britain until the last commercial vineyard was grubbed up near Cardiff in the 1920s. Only after the Second World War did the practice re-emerge, now championed by determined men and women who were convinced that grapes could again be grown here on a com-mercial scale and compete with the best Europe had to offer. Subsequent history has proved them right, and vineyards are now grown happily almost anywhere south of a line drawn between the Wash and Cardiff.

I was captured by the idea of making wine grown from my own grapes and my wife and I began to look for a house that would suit the planting of a vineyard amongst our other requirements. But then life went horribly wrong. Just as we had found the ideal house, our marriage fell apart with a large bang! The marriage was irretrievable and with it died my vision of ever having a vineyard.

But God loves to bring life out of death! Though it was still more than ten years before the vision resurfaced. By then I had been found by Jesus and after several years had met and married my lovely Christian wife Janice. We live in a medium-sized terraced house in Croydon on the southern end of Greater London. When I first came to the house, the garden had been neglected and trampled by children for years! But during the early years of our marriage we tidied up the garden and by 1992 the top half was lawn and the bottom half given over to a vegetable patch. It's a great garden to have. It's seventy-five feet long and the sun rises at the bottom and gives uninterrupted sunshine all day. I cannot say that I am an avid gardener. In fact gardening is a bit of chore sometimes, but I must confess to enjoying the results, and it's a nice feeling to have garden fresh, homegrown vegetables served up with the Sunday roast. One day as I was hoeing in between my rows of cabbages and carrots, the Holy Spirit seemed to nudge me and whisper to my spirit in that rather startling yet casual way He has: "You know Martin," He said, "you could plant a vineyard here." I was staggered. It was so simple yet so explicit. I can honestly say that never once in the previous ten years had I even thought of the possibility, the idea was so dead. I had never even mentioned the idea to Janice. But now as I leaned on my hoe, I could instantly see only vines where moments before had been potatoes and broccoli!

I was so excited, not simply with the idea of an old dream becoming a possibility, but with the thought that my God loved me so much that He wanted to give me the desire of my heart – even when the desire had completely died as far as I was concerned! I had so forgotten it that it would not have mattered to me if no one had ever mentioned it again. When I approached Janice with the idea, I wondered if she would object, but she was more than happy for me to "have a go", in fact she was very encouraging. So the following weeks and months were spent researching how to begin. Little did I know then that God was not just giving me an old desire of my heart, He had His agenda in this vision too! And for Him this was to be a vineyard through which He would speak to me time and time again. You might call it a prophetic vineyard. But then God's really keen on vineyards, after all, He planted one Himself.

Chapter 3

Noah Planted a Vineyard

It's strange how things develop with God isn't it? I know of one preacher who is often quoted as saying that "God does more behind our backs than in front of our faces"! I have to confess that I have found that to be very true. It's as if God has foresight which He is only prepared to give to us as hindsight! I wish He gave it to us sooner. I had no idea when I first became interested in homemade wines that it would lead me to finding out so much about God. I wasn't even a Christian at the time! But God knew the path I was on and was working busily behind my back preparing the ground to speak to me through this wonderful part of His creation years later.

The age between the expulsion of Adam and Eve from the garden of Eden, through the Patriarchs and up to the flood, must have been a quite fascinating period of history to have lived through. The memory of Eden would still be fresh in the minds of Adam and Eve and their family, even though the memory of God's paradise on earth would progressively fade. Some men still sought God and found Him, like Enoch, who is recorded as walking with God before He seemed to simply absorb him into Himself like a sponge absorbs water. But increasingly the majority did not do so, until Noah was found by God to be the only righteous person on earth. Noah, whose name means "rest", is one of the most memorable biblical characters and it's in the story of Noah that we first find a vineyard mentioned in the Bible.

In Genesis we read about Noah getting down to life after the flood. The Word simply says,

> *"Noah began to be a farmer, and he planted a vineyard."*
>
> (Genesis 9:20)

I used to wonder why, when you've just "restarted" the human race on earth again, that you would begin by planting a vineyard. If it was me in that situation I would probably try to be quite practical and start with quick-growing things like lettuces and tomatoes, or cabbages, and then plant things that would take a little longer to mature like potatoes or corn, moving on to the longer-term items like fruit trees. Vines fall into the latter category, yet it was the very first thing Noah planted! Now, of course, that's just my idea. It's me doing what we human beings usually do. It's me using my limited knowledge of growing and life and making my own decision as to what is best based on human logic. It's what gets us into lots of trouble as Christians: we don't ask God what to do and actually He knows best! So what about Noah? Do you think he asked God? The Bible simply says that he planted the vineyard; it does not say that it was his idea. But let's put ourselves in his position and see if it really was his idea.

We know that Noah enjoyed God's grace:

> *"Noah found grace in the eyes of the LORD."*
>
> (Genesis 6:8)

And God said that He found Noah to be,

> *"Righteous before Me in this generation."*
>
> (Genesis 7:1)

Noah was a righteous man, and God was gracious to him. In other words, God was on his side because he sought after Him and honoured Him, even though the world around him was,

> *"Corrupt . . . filled with violence."*
>
> (Genesis 6:11)

Then at the age of 500, God told Noah that because of the world's wickedness He would destroy all flesh on the earth, but that He would save Noah and his family in an ark that Noah was to build . . . and by the way, these are the measurements! I don't know about you, but under the circumstances, I think Noah displayed a quite remarkable level of faith for which he is rightly commended.

> *"By faith Noah, being divinely warned of things not yet seen, moved with godly fear, prepared an ark for the saving of his household, by which he condemned the world and became heir of the righteousness which is according to faith."*
>
> (Hebrews 11:7)

Put another way, Noah's faith in God sustained him for the 100 years it took him to build an ark measuring 450 feet long and 75 feet wide with three decks. That's more than twice as long as the *Cutty Sark* and half as long as the *Queen Mary 1*. Nothing remotely resembling it had ever been seen or built before. It's big even by today's standards and because he saw it through to the end, God called him righteous. Wow! What a testament of faith in action. How well would you or I have done with that task? Can't you just hear the neighbours?

"Are you really sure God told you to do that?" or, "Come off it Noah, you've been building that thing for eighty years now!" People would have tutted behind his back and called it "Noah's Folly"; children would have made up songs about him in the playground (not very nice ones)! And then there would be the nagging doubts of Satan: "Are you sure you got those measurements right? How long do you think it's going to take? Did God really say...?"

And without wishing to make any politically incorrect judgements, I deeply suspect Mrs Noah may have had more than one or two choice words to say on the subject too! Monty Python would have a field day with it. "And another thing, maybe if you didn't spend all your money on that stupid old timber yard of yours in the back garden we could have a decent family holiday like everyone else in the neighbourhood!" or, "I don't know, you just don't seem to have any time left for me and the kids, you're always down the garden banging away on that ark thing of yours" and "We're the laughing stock of the village!"

But through it all he persevered by faith. Imagine what it must have felt like when all those animals turned up at the back door two by two! "Dad! Dad! Two lions and two rhinos have just come up the path and they're trying to get in to your ark!"

And then to be sealed in to the ark, family and animals together, by God Himself. Bang! I would have been petrified! What if the sabre tooth tigers got out? Then there was the rain; it had never rained before! What was it? Would it ever stop? And the screams and calls of all those terrified people outside, banging on the side of the ark to be let in, gradually descending into an eerie quiet broken only by the continuous dripping of the rain, as one by one they all perished. Five months afloat with no sight of land (was the Holy Spirit hovering over these waters too?), and nearly another seven months waiting for the all-clear from God, before going out of the ark onto dry land once more. What an awesome experience, a fantastic, emotional rollercoaster, and what incredible faith!

The first thing Noah did on dry land was to build an altar and sacrifice to the Lord. The last time a sacrifice had been made for mankind was when God Himself slew animals for their skins, with which to cover the shame of Adam and Eve when they sinned in the garden. But now Noah sacrificed to cover the shame of a violent and corrupt generation of which he had been a part, and God honoured his faith and humility with His own promise to Noah. He sealed His promise forever by setting His bow in the sky.

So let me put the question to you: If you had just lived through Noah's last 101 years, what would you do next? What I would most certainly *not do* next is call a family conference and say, "Right, that's the ark thing done and dusted. God's promised never to destroy everyone again, so we can all relax. The animals have all gone so there's nothing much to do or worry about, so what's it to be? Build a house, plant some vegetables or a game of football boys?"

No, I think I would be very much inclined to say, "Thank You for saving us Lord and for Your fantastic promise to us. What should we do now?"

And I have no doubt at all that it was the Lord who said, "Become a farmer and start by planting a vineyard." And so he did.

The landing place God had chosen was of course Mount Ararat at the far eastern end of modern-day Turkey, in the area between the Black Sea and the Caspian Sea. If you're a Christian reading this, it will come as no surprise that it is in this very area that modern viticulturalists confirm that vines as we know them (*vitis vinifera*), first originated and have since spread to all corners of the globe.

God had put Noah in an interesting position. At the beginning of creation He had placed Noah's forefather Adam in the Garden of Eden to cultivate it and to keep it. Here, at the dawn of a new age of life on earth, He told Noah to become a cultivator, to tend plants just like Adam, but was specific in telling him to plant a vineyard.

Why did God tell Noah to plant a vineyard? Why not tomatoes or apple trees? Well one very simple reason is that God has a principle of doing something in the physical realm before He does it in the spiritual realm.

"However, the spiritual is not first, but the natural, and afterward the spiritual."

(1 Corinthians 15:46)

Here, through Noah's obedience, He physically planted a vineyard so that afterwards He could plant a spiritual vineyard and the Scriptures tell us that His spiritual planting was when He brought the Israelites out of Egypt.

"You have brought a vine out of Egypt;
You have cast out the nations, and planted it.
You prepared room for it,
And caused it to take root,
And it filled the land."

(Psalm 80:8–9)

The way a vineyard is planted is paramount to its future health and productivity. Vines are pretty sensitive things and need to be treated sympathetically, even if they are hardier than you might suppose. Most vines will survive temperatures as low as −23 degrees, but planted in the wrong place they will give up quickly enough. Their main disagreement comes when they are planted with their roots too wet or without sufficient drainage. That is one reason why they are often planted on a slope or hillside. God knew just what He was doing when He landed Noah on a mountain.

God likened His people, His Israel, now the Church, to a vineyard. He uses this spiritual analogy for a number of reasons, which we shall explore through the pages of this book, knowing that the primary reason is always to reveal His love to us. By connecting the exodus of Israel with a planting, He is again underlining the association of the exodus with the new start of humanity born through Noah. God is revealing that He is in the business of drawing a people to Himself; it's another new start, separating the righteous from the unrighteous, those who wanted to follow Him from those who were *"corrupt ... filled with violence"*. He was creating a separated people through whom He would reveal Himself to the world. Vineyards have boundaries; they do not spread where they will in an uncontrolled manner. Vineyards are created environments where a number of vines have been collected, planted and nurtured for a purpose. They are hedged about for protection, cultivated and tended for harvest, and looked after with love and commitment, just as God will look after and love His people. The vineyard also takes the name of its owner. God's vineyard doubly reinforces our knowledge of His love for us, because we know this is not a chore or a good idea for Him, but a joy and a pleasure. He is a gardener and delights in the labour of the garden. He is engaging us in a pastime that He loves and is pretty good at!

And still He goes that step further. He has not popped into the local garden centre and picked up whatever vine they happened to have in stock. God has done His homework in the vine business too and picked out the very best vine that money can buy. This is going to be a fantastic vineyard, the envy of the world. Everybody is going to know about God's vineyard and the wine that comes from it.

> *"Now let me sing to my Well-beloved*
> *A song of my Beloved regarding His vineyard:*
> *My Well-beloved has a vineyard*
> *On a very fruitful hill.*
> *He dug it up and cleared out its stones,*
> *And planted it with the choicest vine."*

(Isaiah 5:1–2)

And again,

> *"Yet I had planted you a noble vine,*
> *a seed of highest quality."*

(Jeremiah 2:21)

Did you know that in the world there are something like 8,000 types of vine? Many are completely unsuitable for producing anything, but well over 1,000 vines are now recognised as varieties fit for wine production. But to God the many varieties we cultivate and plant are of little consequence. There is only one vine worth planting. He only wants the best for us. There is no substitute for our relationship with Jesus and we cannot pretend that mixing anything else with Him will work.

The Word of God declares that Jesus is the vine in God's vineyard:

> *"I am the true vine ... "*

(John 15:1)

God is keen to point out to us the definite article in this. God does not want different vine varieties planted in His vineyard.

> *"You shall not sow your vineyard with different kinds of seed, lest the yield of the seed with which you have sown and the fruit of your vineyard be defiled."*

(Deuteronomy 22:9)

There are several principles here. First and foremost, God's message is that there is only one way to Him and that is through Jesus. All routes do not lead to Him. You cannot know the Father unless you know the Son. I am always surprised and saddened when others from major religions tell me they believe Jesus was a good man and a prophet of God. Why then, do they not believe the things He says? *"No one comes to the Father except through Me,"* Jesus declared (John 14:6). Don't blame me, that's what it says in the Bible! God wants us to only have Jesus in the vineyard, no other substitutes for His power or provision. No yoga or meditation to replace Him; no shared services with other religions; no other "words of God" from sources that conflict with the Bible; no other ways to God.

Most of us in the Church would understand that light and dark
don't mix. But there are other more subtle forms in which we
take in species of vines that are not of Jesus. There is, for just one
example, a move in many churches today to become much more
business like, and to present to the world a different face than the
bumbling parish vicar image so often ridiculed by our media.
Clearly the Bible is in agreement with the pursuit of excellence
and expects us to be organised and together:

> "And whatever you do, do it heartily, as to the Lord and not
> to men."
>
> (Colossians 3:23)

But, in an effort to make our churches more business like, many
have looked to the business world for inspiration. However, if we
take business principles too far, will they defile and dilute the
Church, just like mixed vines? We must be so careful not to
sterilize church with business principles to the levels some
businesses do. I spent fifteen years working for a national retailer
and discovered that the overwhelming majority of business
training courses are based on biblical principles. The last course
I attended, for instance, talked about the negative voice that
whispers to our inner self all the time to try to knock us down and
undermine us (sounds a bit like spiritual warfare to me). They
talked about the need to change our current negative behaviour
patterns by understanding where they are rooted in our past
and getting "healed" of those hurts (I could have quoted them
a few chapters of some books on inner healing). We may need,
they suggested, to write a letter to someone from our past,
releasing them from hurting us, or even speaking out loud that
we forgive them! It was like Christianity at work without the
power of Jesus!

The only problem is, although the principles they used had
some truth, they rarely seemed to work that well in practice.
What could be wrong with boosting someone's self-esteem, or

setting them free from rejection or condemnation? I asked the Lord why. His reply was simple as always:

"The business world is motivated by the desire to make more money. The motive in My Kingdom is the free gift of love to draw you closer to Me. The moment your job ceases to have a financial benefit to the company, the company's commitment to you is over. My commitment to you is everlasting."

I believe that's why so many in the workplace are sceptical about such initiatives. They know that underneath, they are simply being made more efficient for the company's benefit and that their own welfare is of little true consequence – there is no such thing as a long-term relationship or loyalty in industry today. These defiling principles must not be allowed to infiltrate the Church. Our motivation must always be love.

When we introduce staff appraisals in our churches, what is our motive? When we send our people on training courses, do we do it with a spirit of blessing for their benefit or condemnation to bring them up to scratch? When we set our budgets do we exclude faith? When we organise our outreach events are we responding to God's priorities for our church, or are we finding an activity to justify ourselves even if we have not heard from Him?

When Jesus faced the rich young man and told him to give away all his money before following Him, the young man left because the "god" of his heart (his money) had been exposed. Jesus knew he had to let go of that god so he could establish Jesus as his God. How many of us would have gone after him and put an arm round his shoulder and said something like, "Oh look now, there's no need to be upset – you don't have to give it all away just yet, and anyway the Lord might change His mind in time. Come and have a cup of tea and we'll talk about it."

Being grafted into the vine of God gives us an altogether different perspective on how we relate to the world around us.

We do not have to work it all out for ourselves. We do not have to be in charge. We have a loving God who has promised to provide everything for us and to bless us at every turn. Being grafted in assumes that the branch so grafted will in future derive its life and strength from the vine, not the other way around. It is no good having our churches planted with the vine of Jesus if we then try to order and govern our churches with something other than His authority and ways.

We must learn to abide in Him, otherwise we will have no fruit, and after all, vineyards are *supposed* to have fruit. The wisdom of God doesn't always look like ours, but it is always the right wisdom. God says that He planted His vineyard with the very best vine – not a mixture. The Church needs to do some weeding!

Chapter 4

Jesus the Choice Vine

When Noah became a farmer and planted his vineyard he must have used vines he had brought with him from before the flood. I do not doubt that when Noah went into the ark he took with him the very best vines he could find. What would you do? You're going on a journey for you don't know how long, to a place you don't know how far away, and you want to take everything that you could possibly need to start all over again. Which vine would you take? It has to be the best one you know. I don't think Noah would have taken the first vine he saw. I'm sure it was the best tasting, most productive variety he knew. Noah probably did not realise he was acting in a "first the physical" context for God Himself, but he undoubtedly was. He brought out of a world of sin and destruction the very choicest vine which he planted on the side of Mount Ararat. Just as Noah had brought out a physical vine, now God brought out a spiritual vine as He brought Israel out of a land of oppression and captivity in Egypt; He too planted the very choicest vine He knew in His vineyard.

Scripture soon tells us that the choicest vine, even the noble vine of Jeremiah 2:21 that God planted in His vineyard, was Jesus. Jesus Himself attested to this in John 15:1 when He declared unequivocally, *"I am the true vine."* But Paul also referred to the fact that Jesus was there with the people that God brought out of Egypt and led into the desert in a quite extraordinary verse:

> *"For they drank of that spiritual Rock that followed them, and that Rock was Christ."*
>
> (1 Corinthians 10:4)

Moses too, as he recounted some of Israel's relational history with God shortly before he died, declared in beautifully poetic verses how God had separated the nations and finding His own portion in a wild and inhospitable place, He had looked after them and led them:

> *"When the Most High divided their inheritance to the nations,*
> *When He separated the sons of Adam,*
> *He set the boundaries of the peoples*
> *According to the number of the children of Israel.*
> *For the LORD's portion is His people;*
> *Jacob is the place of His inheritance.*
>
> *He found him in a desert land*
> *And in the wasteland, a howling wilderness;*
> *He encircled him, He instructed him,*
> *He kept him as the apple of His eye.*
> *As an eagle stirs up its nest,*
> *Hovers over its young,*
> *Spreading out its wings, taking them up,*
> *Carrying them on its wings,*
> ***So the LORD alone led him,***
> *And there was no foreign god with him."*
>
> (Deuteronomy 32:8–12, emphasis added)

How fantastic. God says He planted a vineyard with a choice vine, that the vine was Jesus, and that Jesus was right there in the Old Testament with the children of Israel as they wandered through

the desert for forty years on their way to the land where they
would cease from their wanderings and become permanent
plantings themselves!

In John 15:14 Jesus talked about us being branches that need
to abide in Him. The only way a separate branch can abide in a
vine is to be grafted in. In just this way, all of us come to a time
and place where we exchange our separateness from God for
unity with Him. Here in the wilderness God gave His constant
invitations to the children of Israel to become grafted in. The
whole of His law was centred around blessings for being obedient
and curses for disobedience. By being obedient they would
become grafted into the flow of His blessings. That is why God
had them declare His blessings and curses to one another across
the valley between Mount Gerizim and Mount Ebal.

Grafting in is a conscious action. It doesn't happen naturally or
by chance. Grafting in comes by decision, wounding and
perseverance. The branch that is to be grafted in has some very
limited sustenance within itself, but unless it quickly bonds to the
parent plant and begins to receive nourishment from it, it will fail.
The bonding is done by both parent and branch being wounded
and the two wounds being bound tightly together. What a picture
this is for the Christian! We know that our Lord Jesus Christ
was wounded for our transgressions and that we are healed by
His stripes (Isaiah 53:5). Are you willing, as He is, to have your
wounds bound tightly to Him so you can share in His glorious
resurrection power and love? It's a pretty good deal!

This grafting in is so important for us. Left to our own devices
we can only grow apart from Jesus and develop our own human
spirit. Grafted into Him, we derive life from His life-giving Spirit.
Ephesians 4:3 tells us we all share a unity in the Spirit, even if we
don't all think the same just yet (Ephesians 4:13). This unity in the
Spirit of God gives us the true DNA of Jesus and cannot lie to us
or deceive us. It is the very Spirit of the Lord shared out among
His people as they nestle into Him in true graftedness. Christians
call this grafting process being born again. It's a great phrase,

because it so accurately describes the change that happens when a new and different DNA (Jesus') begins to flow in us. We have a new life source in us, the only one that can change our natural human nature.

We once invited some Brazilian guests to our house for Sunday lunch. Unfortunately, none of us spoke the others' language, so we communicated by signs, drawings and laughter. Eventually they made it known they had to leave and made praying gestures. We all stood in our front room and began to pray for one another in our own languages. We have no idea to this day what they prayed for us, nor, I suspect, have they any idea what we prayed for them. I only know that as we prayed, the Spirit in all of us witnessed so powerfully to the love of the Father, that we all wept for pure joy at being in the presence of others who knew Jesus, who had the same DNA. We simply knew we were all grafted into the same vine.

When God's Word talks about the need not to mix the vines, not only does it speak of Jesus being the only vine to have in our vineyard, it also is a picture that shows us that God plants people in the body where He wants them (1 Corinthians 12:24). Many Christians are in parts of the Body of Christ we think will suit us; we are not there because God has told us that is where He wants us. We are all different and are all called to different emphases in the Kingdom. We all have individuality, which though valuable to the Kingdom and the very stuff God uses with such power in the right place, can be disastrous and divisive in the wrong place.

Imagine a car factory. How many quality cars do you think would come from it if the employees were farmers, airline pilots, shopkeepers, ballet dancers and teachers? Equally, what kind of cars would come out of a factory staffed only by assembly workers, or only by designers? They would spend all their time arguing about what to do next based on their own experience or preference. What is needed is the right balance of strategists, managers, designers, planners, workers, warehousing and logistics experts, assemblers, finishers and sales staff. Then we will get cars from a car factory. And the owner knows the right people to employ. If we want cars from a car factory we must employ car workers, nothing else. No mix of other workers will have the results we want. But beloved, many of our churches are staffed with all manner of imbalanced giftings. Some want to make this fruit, some another. Of what use is that to the Vinedresser? Does He want mixed bunches of different grapes? What will the wine taste like? The wine of many of our churches tastes bitter and unrefined because we have mixed vines vying for position and prominence. We have not understood that God has a diversified economy throughout His Church and that we as individuals are specifically designed to fit specific work situations. It matters where God has called us to be.

The Bible makes mention of at least two other vines apart from Jesus. Both could have shared all the blessings of being grafted in, but chose other routes.

> *"For their vine is the vine of Sodom."*
>
> (Deuteronomy 32:32)

Sodom, you will recall, was the town in the plain of Jordan that Lot, who was a righteous man, decided to take as his inheritance when the land became too small for both him and Abram (Genesis 13:12). Everyone knows that Sodom was one of the most wicked places on earth, but all that could have changed with Lot's presence amongst them. However, the inhabitants chose wickedness instead.

> *"She [Sodom] and her daughter had pride, fullness of food, and abundance of idleness; neither did she strengthen the hand of the poor and needy. And they were haughty and committed abomination before Me; therefore I took them away as I saw fit."*
>
> (Ezekiel 16:49–50)

Jeremiah 48:32 mentions the other named vine, the vine of Sibmah. This was the land that was originally the home of Sihon, king of the Amorites, but it was taken by Moses and given to Reuben as his inheritance, although it eventually reverted to the Moabites. They too could have been grafted in to all the blessings of the true vine but instead incurred the judgement of God

> *"Because he* [Moab] *exalted himself against the LORD."*
> (Jeremiah 48:42)

As the Bible mentions these two alternative vines we should heed its warnings. Both Sodom and Moab saw fit to elevate themselves above the Lord. Setting our human wisdom, our thinking, our strategies or plans, our imaginings above the wisdom of God has but one end – expulsion from the presence of God and ultimately, destruction.

Lucifer, who was once the one who covered the very throne of God with worship, succumbed to that same pride and found himself hurled to the earth where he has never stopped trying to get us to adopt the same view.

> *"How you are fallen from heaven,*
> *O Lucifer, son of the morning!*
> *How you are cut down to the ground,*
> *You who weakened the nations!*
> *For you have said in your heart:*
> *'I will ascend into heaven,*
> *I will exalt my throne above the stars of God . . .'"*
> (Isaiah 14:12–13)

He even tried to get Jesus to bow down before him, but Jesus countered him from Scripture, as we should, by quoting,

> *"You shall worship the LORD your God, and Him only shall you serve."*
> (Luke 4:8)

This attitude of servanthood displayed by Jesus was not new. He had been with the Father and the Spirit before "in the beginning" and never dreamt of setting Himself higher than God the Father, but instead thought it much better to be His servant. As a result He suddenly found Himself stripped of His godly magnificence and crying as a little human baby.

> *"Let this mind be in you which was also in Jesus Christ, who, being in the form of God, did not consider it robbery to be equal with God, but made Himself of no reputation, taking the form of a bondservant, and coming in the likeness of men. And being found in appearance as a man, He humbled Himself and became obedient to the point of death, even the death of the cross."*
>
> (Philippians 2:5–8)

Jesus, unfortunately for Lucifer but fortunately for us, knew His Scripture better, and knew that He was God's vine. The prophecy of Jotham had also foretold His response:

> *"Then the trees said to the vine,*
> *'You come and reign over us!'*
> *But the vine said to them,*
> *'Should I cease my new wine,*
> *Which cheers both God and men,*
> *And go to sway over trees?'"*
>
> (Judges 9:12–13)

Closer inspection of Scripture reveals an emphasis of the Holy Spirit that again steers us inexorably in the direction of Jesus as the only vine worth considering. Whilst the Old Testament contains some forty-five references to vineyards and twelve references to vines, the New Testament has not one plural reference to either, underlining for us that the New Covenant is only concerned with one vine, Jesus, and one vineyard, the Church.

Two further vineyard stories in the Word of God give us

greater insight into the characteristics of God's vine, Jesus. The first, in the Old Testament in 1 Kings 21, is a prophetic story that foreshadowed the end of the life of Jesus. A man named Naboth had a pleasant vineyard right next to King Ahab's palace. Ahab liked the look of Naboth's vineyard so much that he determined to have it for himself. So he made Ahab an attractive offer, either the full monetary value or another vineyard to replace it. But Naboth had inherited the vineyard from his father and he simply didn't want it to go out of the family. Many of us know how he felt. We may not have a vineyard, but perhaps we have granny's engagement ring or great-granddad's pocket watch. There's no way we would think of parting with such things because they are so precious to us. We want our children to have the same inheritance and enjoy it as we have. So it was with Naboth.

Ahab was upset. In fact, he was so upset he had not got what he wanted that he behaved like a spoiled brat. He went to bed with a miserable face and wouldn't eat his tea! His wife Jezebel noticed all this and asked Ahab what the matter was. She was angry that the king had let a subject refuse him and she devised a scheme to get the vineyard for her husband, despite Naboth's refusal.

She had Naboth set up at a public banquet by two scoundrels who testified falsely that Naboth had blasphemed God and the king. Naboth was instantly found guilty. The punishment for his crime was death by stoning and there was no court of appeal. The sentence was carried out immediately and poor Naboth was stoned to death. Ahab eventually took the now ownerless vineyard for his own possession.

Not a nice story if you happened to be Naboth, but I am glad it is recorded in the Bible because it reveals the heart of God in such an open and tender-hearted way. Naboth, of course, is used as a picture to show us what Jesus would do to protect His inheritance. Jesus came as Head or Owner of the Church, the vineyard, and was, like Naboth, unjustly accused of blasphemy. When Jesus was asked, *"Are You the Christ, the Son of the Blessed?"* by the chief priest, He replied with open candour, *"I am"* (Mark 14:62).

In other words, He replied using the same phrase that God had used when He revealed Himself to Moses – the holy name of God – I AM.

It was enough for the Pharisees to be assured that Jesus was indeed a blasphemer. Alas, they did not recognise He was speaking the truth. His punishment was death at the hands of the Roman occupiers. Our God died out of passion that He might share His inheritance with us, His Church.

The second story is in Luke 20 in the New Testament and concerns a vineyard that had been leased to others. Unfortunately the owner lived a long way away and so sent servants to collect what was due to him. The tenants sent these servants away with a few bruises and broken bones; they even killed some, until finally the owner sent his own son. Those leasing the vineyard thought that if they killed the owner's son, the man would forget about them and they would end up owning the vineyard themselves. The story ends at that point, simply asking us the rhetorical question, "What will the owner do when he does come back?" It's obvious that he will destroy those who killed his son. This too is a picture of Jesus coming to claim His place amongst His people after God has sent countless prophets to her, only to be abused and martyred. It shows us the other side of the compassionate-hearted God who will die rather than give up His inheritance – the heart of a God who can be pushed too far and who will eventually exact a judgement on those who flaunt His authority.

In many ways these two aspects of the heart of God are not new to us. The pages of Old and New Testaments are full of such judgement and compassion. However, we would more usually expect to find the compassion in the New Testament and the judgement in the Old Testament. Here the opposite is the case, as if to remind those who dare to disregard the authority of God that our God is, *". . . the same yesterday, today, and forever"* (Hebrews 13:8).

Nevertheless, the two stories combine to picture for us a God who will die for us, knowing that by death God's harvest will be reaped. Jesus Himself told us,

> *"Most assuredly, I say to you, unless a grain of wheat falls into the ground and dies, it remains alone; but if it dies, it produces much grain."*
>
> (John 12:24)

Truly, here was a man who practised what He preached. Yet He understood the principle of death and harvest and now, because of the sacrifice of Jesus the vine, there is a sure promise of the harvest of the great vine of the earth.

Chapter 5

Vineyards of Desire

God does nothing by chance. Everything He does is for a purpose. The Bible tells the story of God's relationship with His vineyard from the moment He planted it until that moment some time in the future when He will harvest its crop. When we understand that He is talking to us about the Church, much of it makes for cautious reading, though in our caution, we should remember that God's judgements come upon us less out of God's desire to give us a hard smack, than because "that's the way He made it all to work".

The vineyard is not only something God desired for Himself, but is also to the heart of man, something to be desired, a possession that gives much pleasure. The Bible is full of it. Should we be fortunate enough to find a wife of good repute, she works to use her profits to plant a vineyard and this will bless her husband (Proverbs 31:16). In Solomon's time there was peace, such that every man dwelt under his own vine (1 Kings 4:25). The Shulamite in Song of Songs 2:11–13 encourages the Beloved to get up early and come with her to the vineyard because they are so delightfully fragrant in the spring. Have you ever thought that God gets great pleasure from His vineyard too? He does, after all, describe Himself as a Gardener (He planted Eden) and specifically a Vinedresser (John 15; Isaiah 27:2). The first year my few vines fruited I was in the vineyard all the time I could manage and I used to think that God must be like this with us when He sees us making fruitful progress. He'll be right there with the cloud of witnesses cheering us on and encouraging us every day. It was simply so exciting to see the grapes changing from stage to stage as I watched the years of patience and training finally paying off. I also readily confess to talking to the vines in the name of Jesus and encouraging them to greater fruitfulness!

When I first planted our few vines, my wife Janice was very gracious about the idea, but seemed keen to let me know how much time "my" vines were taking up and how much money was being spent on "my" vines (meaning me!). But the moment recognisable grapes first appeared on those plants in the third growing year, a surprising change happened to her point of view. Suddenly, she wanted to know if I had sprayed "her" vines lately and when people came to the house, she wanted to show them "her" vines! Something happened in her heart to unite her with the vineyard and the vines, something that has never left. She was excited over the prospect of harvest where none could previously be seen.

We have one large vine trained over a pergola. We sit under its shade in the summer and eat and drink with our family and friends. As the summer weeks roll by we delight to watch the grapes first appear as tiny hard green dots, which gradually swell and hang down with their own weight to ripen in September and October into wonderful tight black bunches. Recently, we developed a patio area at the far end of our garden beyond the main vineyard. Here we sit, a high old brick wall at our backs, enclosed at the sides by our neighbour's and our summerhouses, the vines before us. We are no longer in the city, we are in a vineyard and all is well! The peace there is fantastic and like those in Solomon's time, we derive hours of delight just by being amongst the vines. But God has something even better for us in eternity.

"For behold, I create new heavens and a new earth;
And the former shall not be remembered or come to mind . . .
They shall plant vineyards and eat their fruit."

(Isaiah 65:17, 21)

It excites me that we will no longer remember what it was like in vineyards on this earth. I can only assume that God will create something that we will understand as a vineyard that will be so much better than that which we now know, with fruit so much juicier, as to render it completely obsolete in our minds!

I wonder, since the vineyard God talks of is His Church – a place of great relational value to us, both with God and with one another – whether what He has in store for us in heaven is also a relational experience? We already know that then we will know Him as fully as He now knows us, so there is a good possibility that we will know each other in a much deeper way than we do here. My wife hates the idea of us not being married in heaven, but I contend that if we are one flesh on earth, in heaven we will be something even closer.

In any case, I can hardly wait. There is something very special about the experience one can have in a vineyard that you don't get from other crops. Growing up in Lincolnshire I can confidently testify that a field of sugar beet holds very little romance, as do potatoes or kale! But whenever my wife and I travel in France, there is always a thrill when we come to the vineyards and an equal and opposite sadness when we leave them behind. They are so beautifully kept. In fact it's rare to see an old, overgrown or messy vineyard. Along many of the roads that pass them, the owners proudly display their family name on wrought iron arches over the gateway and some have rose bushes planted at the end of the rows. There is a real pride in making their vineyard and the resulting wine something to shout about. God also desires the very best from His vineyard. He does not want B, C, D or plain pass level Christianity; He wants A level Christianity every time.

God expects to have a great harvest from His vineyard, as we do from ours, and He's just as disappointed as we are when the grape harvest fails. Unfortunately God's original desire for His vineyard to flourish has not yet happened because of the Church's disobedience. Have you ever seen a small child throw a temper tantrum in a public place and watched a patient, but harassed, parent trying to placate the child with love? I sometimes think we are very much like that in the Church. We seem at times to want to do everything and anything except that which our Father really wants us to do. And though our Father loves us to "little mint-balls" (as a friend of mine says!), He still calls what we do disobedience, because it's not what He wants us to do. Churches are great at filling the time with good activities, but we must get into the habit of asking God whether they are the activities He wants us to do. It's not that so much of what we do is bad, but it may simply not be what He wants. Now, however hard we try to believe something else, this is not without consequence, and the pages of the Bible are full of warnings we should take notice of.

Hosea bewailed the fate of Israel saying,

> *"Israel empties his vine;*
> *He brings forth fruit for himself."*
>
> (Hosea 10:1)

He then goes on to list Israel's faults, which include double-mindedness, no fear of the Lord, rejection of authority, speaking unwise words and craving for the gods of the past. What an indictment on the Church, an indictment that went further to a judgement that would see Israel taken into captivity in 722 BC.

Joel used the vine as a picture of the southern kingdom of Judah when he foresaw their captivity many years before the event.

> *"For a nation has come up against My land,*
> *Strong, and without number . . .*
> *He has laid waste My vine."*
>
> (Joel 1:6–7)

Judgement was coming to the Church. No wonder Isaiah prophesied the Lord's heart when he said,

> *"Now let me sing to my Well-beloved*
> *A song of my Beloved regarding His vineyard:*
>
> *My Well-beloved has a vineyard*
> *On a very fruitful hill.*
> *He dug it up and cleared out its stones,*
> *And planted it with the choicest vine.*
> *He built a tower in its midst,*
> *And also made a winepress in it;*
> *So He expected it to bring forth good grapes,*
> *But it brought forth wild grapes.*
>
> *And now, O inhabitants of Jerusalem and men of Judah,*
> *Judge, please, between Me and My vineyard.*
> *What more could have been done to My vineyard*
> *That I have not done in it?*
> *Why then, when I expected it to bring forth good grapes,*
> *Did it bring forth wild grapes?*
> *And now, please let Me tell you what I will do*
>   *to My vineyard:*
> *I will take away its hedge, and it shall be burned;*
> *And break down its wall, and it shall be trampled down.*
> *I will lay it waste;*
> *It shall not be pruned or dug,*
> *But there shall come up briers and thorns.*
> *I will also command the clouds*
> *That they rain no rain on it.'*
> *For the vineyard of the* LORD *of hosts is the house of Israel,*
> *And the men of Judah are His pleasant plant.*
> *He looked for justice, but behold, oppression;*
> *For righteousness, but behold, a cry for help."*

(Isaiah 5:1–7)

Do you hear the anguish in God's heart for His Church? He has done everything needed to bring forth good fruit and He expects, as would any farmer, to get a good crop from us. One that will show the unsaved of the world the beauty of life knowing Him. But in all this God's purpose is that we repent and return to Him.

It seems that most of the problems with the Church are at root simple ones. God's answers usually are too. It seems that we like to take control for ourselves and function out of our own understanding. But as I read the Scriptures it is clear that God wants to be in control.

When I first came out of secular work and into full-time ministry, I asked the Lord what His plan was for my life. He told me, "My plan for your life is that you should seek Me each day for My plan for that day."

Like most of us do, I argued with God. "No Lord, You don't understand, I need a short-term plan, a medium-term plan, and I want to know where You are taking me long term." His reply took me from my place of arrogance and gently deposited me where I should be, dependent on Him:

> "If I gave you a six-month plan for your life you would dash off and work out how you think it should be done and never speak to Me in the process. Now, when you can seek Me for My plan each day, I will teach you how to seek Me for My plan for each hour of your life!"

Needless to say, I am still being taught! But the more I let Him have real control in my life, the more I find the goodness of God flowing in my life. I am convinced this is a principle God wants in His Church. God wants us in a place of rest so He can work. He says things like,

> *"I will build My church."*
>
> (Matthew 16:18)

And,

> *"And I, if I am lifted up from the earth, will draw all peoples to Myself."*

(John 12:32)

And,

> *"Seek first the kingdom of God and His righteousness, and all these things shall be added to you."*

(Matthew 6:33)

There are countless examples of God telling us that we cannot do it by ourselves (sometimes we don't even know what "it" really is!) and that He has to be the One giving the orders. He once chided me for trying to be too complex with the words, "You have no idea what complexity is!" which coming from the Creator of the universe and all matter, bears some thinking about! Point taken again, Lord! This does not mean at all that we sit back and do nothing, but that we only "do" when He says so. Remember that we are human beings, not human doings. The great Argentinean revival that has been continuing for over fifty years, began when an evangelist used all his considerable administrative powers to organise a two-week crusade to which not one person came! Having reached the end of himself and his ideas of how to reach the Argentine nation, he got round to asking God what the problem was. "You are," was God's response. Not a nice thing to hear, but applicable to us all at times. God then told him to pray every day and not to go out and try to evangelise. Two years of obedience later, the Holy Spirit rushed in and filled the evangelist and three others one evening and the revival started which continues to this day. I think that's a much better way of doing Church than our usual experience.

There's a wonderful prayer in the Bible which encapsulates God's desire to be in control of His own people:

"Shepherd your people with your staff,
   the flock of your inheritance,
which lives by itself in a forest,
   in fertile pasturelands.
Let them feed in Bashan and Gilead
   as in days long ago."

(Micah 7:14 NIV)

And the Lord answers,

"As in the days when you came out of Egypt,
   I will show them my wonders."

(Micah 7:15 NIV)

The prayer recognises the Church is in a mess. What on earth is a flock of sheep doing milling about in a forest when they should be in the green pastures that are all around? But what a great prayer to ask the Lord to shepherd us out and to cause us to find the very best pasture available. God's reply is so relevant to us today, because His answer to this prophetic prayer of Micah is that He will show "them" – in other words a people yet to come, which can be us – His wonders. I want to see the power of God flowing through the Church don't you?

The good answer to that is that God has promised He will lead us and restore us to what we are supposed to be. Almost all of the prophets, whilst warning of or pronouncing judgement on the Church, also talk of the eventual restoration of the Church, which will culminate in the Lord Jesus presenting the Church to the Father as the fulfilment of His word, *"Let Us make man in Our image"* (Genesis 1:26), as the Bride of Christ without spot or wrinkle.

He promises that,

"As yet the vine ... have not yielded fruit. But from this day [figuratively from the day we repent and turn wholeheartedly towards the Lord] *I will bless you."*

(Haggai 2:19)

And when we are obedient to God and cease robbing Him,

> *". . . I will rebuke the devourer for your sakes,*
> *So that he will not destroy the fruit of your ground.*
> *Nor shall the vine fail to bear fruit for you in the field."*

(Malachi 3:11)

> *"For the seed shall be prosperous,*
> *The vine shall give its fruit,*
> *The ground shall give her increase,*
> *And the heavens shall give their dew —*
> *I will cause the remnant of this people*
> *To possess all these."*

(Zechariah 8:12)

God only desires that we allow Him to be Lord.

Chapter 6

Cooperating with the Vinedresser

As the Israelites entered the Promised Land, God commanded them to remind one another of the blessing and curse attached to be obedient or disobedient to Him. One group shouted the blessing for obedience from Mount Gerizim, which included a general blessing on all the produce of the land:

> *"Blessed shall you be in the city, and blessed shall you be in the country. Blessed shall be the fruit of your body, the produce of your ground . . ."*
>
> (Deuteronomy 28:3–4)

The remaining half of Israel shouted the curse for disobedience from Mount Ebal across to Mount Gerizim and part of the curse was specific to vineyards:

> *"You shall plant vineyards and tend them, but you shall neither drink of the wine nor gather the grapes; for the worms shall eat them."*
>
> (Deuteronomy 28:39)

This warning not only draws our attention to the obvious, but because God pictures the Church as His vineyard, reminds us that when the Church is disobedient it will not fruit. God warns us of the consequence of not being obedient as part of the process by which He is drawing us to Himself to spend eternity with Him.

> *"You have seen what I did to the Egyptians, and how I bore you on eagles' wings and brought you to Myself. Now therefore, if you will indeed obey My voice and keep My covenant, then you shall be a special treasure to Me above all people; for all the earth is Mine. And you shall be to Me a kingdom of priests and a holy nation."*
>
> (Exodus 19:4–6)

If we want to be a special treasure to God, and I certainly do, then we should heed the warnings of the vine and learn from the way the Lord speaks of it. Giving up our control of events and life is central to how God wants our relationship to function. He is God, we are men: He is the Vinedresser, we are the vines grafted into Jesus. Cooperation with the Vinedresser is paramount to the health and fruitfulness of vines. Another word for cooperation is obedience. Don't let us be too negative though, for there are many positives, and the overriding message is that the Church's harvest will eventually be full and bountiful. However, the time span between "today" and that harvest depends not so much on the Lord as on how we respond to Him. When our vines fail we do something about it to restore their vigour and fruitfulness. In extreme circumstances we may even replant. God reacts in the same way. In the Old Testament this process is usually called "judgement", whereas in the New Testament we better understand it as the hand of the Father bringing discipline to us and showing us through it that He is treating us as sons. God's motive is that He is working to get His vineyard into quality grape production.

We have seen in a previous chapter how God gave the Israelites the best possible start by planting them with the choicest vine. It could all have been so very different for them. Had Israel come out of Egypt and trusted God they could have been in the

Promised Land within two weeks, but their constant mistrust, grumbling and disobedience kept them in the desert for forty years until all except Joshua and Caleb remained of those who had come out of captivity. Yet again God had to start from the beginning as He had done with Noah. God's remedy for our persistent failure to act in faith and obedience for the promises of God, is eventually to use someone else! It is a great mistake to suppose that God has unlimited patience with us. His patient love for us indeed never runs out, but we can run out of time and then the mantle falls to another. We do not have the luxury of immortality just yet – an infinity of time that prompted Sir Winston Churchill to comment that he would spend the first five million years painting the colour blue!

If successive generations of vines are to become more fruitful than preceding generations, something must change. Soil content or feeding programme, general health or climate. The same is true for younger Christians. Each generation of the Church must learn that they cannot afford the time to make the same mistakes as older Christians and expect to achieve different results. There is a deception of the enemy prevalent in the spirit of this age which presupposes that youth alone possesses dynamic vigour, creativity, vision and truth, and that age is redundant, in some cases even before it has had time to mature! Vines do not reach instant maturity like some annual seed plants which spring up to full stature in a single season, seed, wither and then die. The vines in my garden are eleven years old and have reached maturity, though it took at least four years and then some, to get to where they are now with thick supporting stems, deeply rooted and able to withstand the rigours of the driest summer. Western culture does not have time for maturity, seeming to want everything instantly on demand. The Church must vigorously oppose this spirit and instead pray fervently for the release of the spirit of Elijah, to infuse our generational relationships with hearts of fatherhood and sonship.

The replacement generation of Israel preparing to enter the Promised Land were commanded by Moses to shout out the blessing and curse for obedience and disobedience. Obedience and disobedience reveal the heart of the father–son relationship. Where there is obedience, the increase of the government of the kingdom of God will flow from father to son, because that is the way God has made it to work. There is no discussion, no barter; the son is obedient to the father. The reverse also is true: where there is disobedience there is not true sonship. Jesus made it very plain in His story about the two sons who were asked to go to work in the father's vineyard. The true son was the one who understood his relationship with his father and eventually decided, even against his own desires, to be obedient to the wishes of his father – unlike his brother who declared his willingness straight away, but actually never got around to the obedient action that needed to follow his words. Our hearts are revealed by our actions not our words alone (Matthew 21:28–41). Neither should we allow ourselves the freedom to believe that we will get a better reward for length of service! There are no long-service stripes in God's army; the wages are the same whenever you start. Salvation, eternal life and an inheritance with Christ! Those are our wages for obedience, so the sooner we start, the sooner we enter into the blessings (Matthew 20:1–8).

God tells us some of the things that go wrong in the vineyard through His prophets and again, His words make for sobering reading. Answering Jeremiah's question of the Lord, in essence asking why it seems that He blesses the wicked but not the Church, the Lord replies:

> "Many rulers have destroyed My vineyard,
> They have trodden My portion underfoot;
> They have made My pleasant portion a desolate wilderness.
> They have made it desolate;
> Desolate, it mourns to Me;
> The whole land is made desolate,
> Because no one takes it to heart."

> (Jeremiah 12:10–11)

In the translation above the Bible talks of the problem being rooted in "many rulers" and I have used that translation to break the news gently that a more apt and proper translation of the original word "rulers" is actually pastors. *Strong's Concordance* says that the root of the word means "to tend a flock", so the translation "rulers" must be seen in that context – in other words "rulers who tend flocks", or "shepherds" or "pastors". This is not an opportunity for all disaffected members of churches to jump up and shout, "I told you the pastor was wrong!" Far from it, but it is a place for the Church as a whole to lament and repent, because God says that this is everyone's responsibility. "No one takes it to heart" is not aimed only at shepherds. The original problem may well be that pastors have not pastored as well as they might or provided the leadership in the Church that could have been given and this has resulted in the Church becoming desolate. However, and here's the rub, no one else seems to be bothered.

A while ago, I went to a wedding in a traditional church with a traditional robed minister, choir and all the usual forms of service you would anticipate, but my spirit was troubled all the way through. Something was not right, but I could not put my finger on it. Then, right at the end, the officiating minister pronounced his blessing on the happy couple. But instead of blessing in the name of the Father, Son and Holy Spirit, he blessed them in the name of "father sun, mother moon and the bounty of daughter earth"! What was he doing? That kind of shepherding will leave God's Church desolate! All the more so as long as the people he's shepherding tolerate his waywardness.

It's a sad fact, and disobedience to God's Word, that parts of the Church are happy to let things like that slip by and say nothing, yet such an incident reveals so much more about the underlying beliefs being preached. It is irrelevant that 99% of the service could not be faulted for the words that were spoken; it is enough that those few words of blessing reveal a theology that does not serve one God alone. This is "mixing our vines" and whilst it may seem severe, there is no room for a gospel that dilutes the Word of God to satisfy our whims, fantasies, political correctness, or the out and out lies of the enemy. Shepherds who preach doctrines that conflict with the Word of Scripture, like the deregulation of homosexuality from sin status to non-sin status, or saying that it does not matter if we believe in the resurrection or a virgin birth or not, need our prayers that they will meet with the living Jesus through His revelation, but should not be tolerated in positions as leaders of God's flock. These doctrines only support a false Christianity with a wishy-washy love that develops doctrines to provide what their "itching ears" long to hear (2 Timothy 4:3). True Christianity does not change to suit society, but is constantly revealed as relevant to society by a loving God.

The Church is supposed to be the most radical group of people on the face of the earth. We are designed to be a people through whom God reveals Himself to the world. God does not change the way He is or the way He deals with us. His Word is the same yesterday, today and forever and He will not work outside it. Collectively, shepherds and flock alike, have the responsibility to ensure that the Church remains true to God's Word. The gospel is pretty simple really. It's all in the book; anything which is not in the book, or conflicts with the spirit of what is in the book, is not the gospel. Shepherds need as much, if not more, accountability than sheep, because whatever they say and do influences so many others. We are so often ready, with our soft interpretation of love, to accept things we should quickly reject. God calls them little foxes. We tolerate the things which in the end destroy us.

> "Catch us the foxes,
> The little foxes that spoil the vines,
> For our vines have tender grapes."
>
> (Song of Songs 2:15)

Grapes, the fruit of vines, are easily damaged at any stage of their development. Though the foxes may be little, they can cause enormous damage by their rough and tumbling amongst the vines.

A seemingly small word or act that conflicts with Scripture is non-cooperation with the Vinedresser. Obedience and cooperation require a structure of authority to comply with, and we will only find out if we are under authority when it asks us to do something we would rather not! On the whole, the Church tends towards a style of leadership that is weak and more concerned with maintaining the status quo than with creating clear lines of communication and authority.

It is clear that when the authority of God is restored to the Church, God delegates His authority to godly men who will oversee the work that He wants to build. It's back to the shepherds theme: God supplies His own shepherds, more anointed than appointed! During Israel's greatest years under King David, the Bible shows us that in the organisation and social structure he brought to the nation, the administration of vineyards was an important part.

> *"And Shimei the Ramathite was over the vineyards, and Zabdi the Shiphmite was over the produce of the vineyards for the supply of wine."*
>
> (1 Chronicles 27:27)

It is also a part of the restoration of the Church. We read in the reign of King Uzziah, who was a godly king who sought the Lord all the days of his life, and restored the nation to right standing with God that

> *". . . he also had farmers and vinedressers in the mountains and in Carmel, for he loved the soil."*
>
> (2 Chronicles 26:10)

If at first the need to submit ourselves to authority and be obedient seems a hard requirement for the Church, consider that

His remedy for the spiritual Church is not only that He will do the leading, instructing and guiding, but also that He will change our hearts from hearts of stone towards Him, into hearts of flesh with His law written on them, so that we can and want to cooperate to Him. He tells us He will make the complete "once for all" sacrifice that will enable us to come back to relationship with Him, He reveals Jesus as the true vine of God, and that we must be grafted into Him. Then we will succour the true DNA of Jesus that will affect that change of heart and enable us to draw close to Him. God, through His love for us, does it all.

Left to ourselves we vines are ill-disciplined. The only way for the vineyard to prosper is for it to cooperate with the Vinedresser, right from the first moment of preparation and planting, through establishment and fruiting, and on towards glorious harvest.

Chapter 7

Preparation and Establishment

Solomon, the wisest man who has ever lived, pursued wisdom in many different ways. One was to plant vineyards and observe what he might learn from them. Out of his observations came this proverb:

> *"I went by the field of the lazy man,*
> *And by the vineyard of the man devoid of understanding;*
> *And there it was, all overgrown with thorns;*
> *Its surface was covered with nettles;*
> *Its stone wall was broken down.*
> *When I saw it, I considered it well;*
> *I looked on it and received instruction:*
> *A little sleep, a little slumber,*
> *A little folding of the hands to rest;*
> *So shall your poverty come like a prowler,*
> *And your need like an armed man."*
>
> (Proverbs 24:30–34)

It is surprising how quickly vines grow once they spring from their dormant winter state. Leave them for a couple of days and you have a backlog of work to catch up on and trouble is upon you. A little folding of the hands and you are easily behind with the work.

During the first year of planting, vines are not allowed to crop and are restricted to growing only one cane about four feet long. All other growth is stopped. This encourages the energy generated by the plant into producing and developing a strong healthy root system without being distracted by other things like producing fruit. Without good roots the plant will not thrive. Without roots the plant cannot reach down for the sustenance it needs for growth. Like the house built on sand in the parable, when the storms come it will have no stability. If fruit is allowed in the first year, too much energy is taken from the plant and not only will the fruit be unrefined and useless, but the plant will be weakened and will take years to recover its fruit bearing potential. Many who become Christians fall at this very first hurdle. The vine is a plant that does not thrive left to its own devices. It only thrives when someone takes an interest in it to prune, teach, guide and nurture it. Many Christians think they can "go it alone" and fail in isolation.

Left to its own devices, the vine would become a large plant with branches all over the place that were weak and unfruitful with only the prospect of yet more unfruitfulness. A rigorous and severe pruning is the only thing that will get it back on the right track. There are such lessons for us to learn here. Sadly, many of our new Christians end up like the unfruitful vine and some even fade away altogether.

I have to say that I am not a fan of those who advocate harnessing and promoting the energy of new Christians as a model with which to motivate the Church to reach the world. This immature vigour will, on the whole, not sustain the young Christian and often shows the Church to the world as ill-disciplined (the word means not discipled!) and impotent. The results are all too often disempowering for the Christian and off-putting and distancing for the non-Christian. Driven by the energy found through meeting Jesus, young believers want to charge off to change the world in an instant. This folly often leaves people burnt out, disillusioned or backslidden, or else unwittingly recruited by the enemy of our souls into Jezebel-type rebellion. How often do you hear the cry, "Yes but, God told me to ..."? Spirits unable to be guided by the rod and staff of submission and obedience to the authorities that God provides for us in the anointed ministries of the Church, end up only being able to take a "first year cane" of religious fervour to the world, for they have not yet learned the process of fruiting and have no sweetness or depth of mature wine to give.

The counsel of Scripture is always a patient one and I have never seen God bless the impatience of man, however fervent and well-intentioned. Often He will allow us to move with our impatience, but only so we fall over and learn that His patience is better! Moses was forty years in the desert learning how to shepherd sheep before God allowed Him to shepherd His people. Joseph spent years in prison and captivity learning that God was in control not him. Paul made tents for ten years after he got knocked off his horse. Our roots, our foundations, are so important. We should heed the warning of Scripture:

> "If the foundations are destroyed,
> What can the righteous do?"
>
> (Psalm 11:3)

Well-established vine roots burrow deep into the ground. It is not uncommon for vine roots to burrow up to fourteen metres into the earth! That's perhaps ten feet deeper than the height of an average two-story house. But down in these depths is where they not only find nourishment, but also water that will sustain the plant in times of drought. Times of drought for un-rooted Christians are times of great danger and potential destruction, and a major factor in why so many either fall away or retreat into formatted religious safety or passivity. As far as the enemy is concerned, his job is done; they are no longer any threat to him as long as they remain religious or passive or both.

At the end of the vine's first year what has been grown is cut right back to just two buds – perhaps four inches of wood. From each bud will grow a cane in the following season. Both canes will need support as they grow, but again, even in the second year, no fruit is allowed. Patience! The vine is still being established. However, one of these two canes will bear fruiting rods in the following year. This is the year of preparation for fruit in the third year, albeit only a half crop as the plant is gradually eased into fruiting. Three years before any fruit and only half the potential at that! Yet that is God's patient way. And it is also time to look even further ahead, as the second of these two canes will be pruned back to two buds at the end of the second year to provide a further two canes in the third year. These two "third year" canes will then provide the fruiting rods for the fourth year. If this pattern is established, the plant will regularly crop to its potential and those of the prevailing conditions of the year.

What fine principles to understand when nurturing in the Church. The little growth we are allowed in our first year is cut right back to only two potential growth points, yet it seems it is common practice to encourage young converts to engage with the Church wherever and whenever they can. Herein, of course, lie two major issues for the Church. First, as we have previously discussed, there is a need for the hearts of sons who are willing to defer to mature leaders, and second, there is a need for the Church to develop those mature leaders that can recognise and channel potential as a father lovingly guiding a son.

Sons rarely at first see their future with the same clarity as their father. I want to make it clear that I am not advocating anything remotely approaching what happened in the heavy shepherding movement of the sixties and seventies, but to emphasise that in the early years a parent will have a more intense guiding role than later. Relationships based on the loving nurture of God, rather than positional dictates, survive the changes and pressure growth

places upon them and gradually substitute reliance for honour, a
quality too infrequently seen in our churches. The vine knows
something of its potential and purpose and has great desire and
fervour. The Father knows how to help it develop and channel
those energies and desires into the production of fruit.

Fortunately for us, our Father in heaven is the Vinedresser and
He prunes and trains us so that we bear much fruit. It is often said
that God and Satan are both interested in the Christian and that
both want him dead! Not much of a choice on the surface, but
whilst Satan is intent on imposing destruction on us so that our
lives are unproductive or ended, God is after our willing self-
destruction. That is, the destruction of my self so that His self, His
life, His desires, His plans, His ideas, His character, His goodness
and His love and His mercy can flow through me. Quite a
difference. Often it seems we end up fighting what we think must
be the devil, only to find that it was God all the time trying to get
us to take some part of our self-life to the cross for crucifixion.

How hard a pruning that is to bear, yet the vine suffers it every
year, to be cut back to only two of perhaps a dozen or more
canes, both of which are then bent horizontally across the
training and support wires. A willing sacrifice? Before bending,
the canes are upright where they have been aiming for the light
all summer long. Now, here in the depth of winter, when all sign
of growth has gone, when leaves lie dead on the ground, when
the energy of growth is laid dormant by the frosts, then is the
time of pruning. Christian, if you want more fruit in your life,
note well the time of pruning. It will not be when you have so
much growth that you will not miss the odd bit of wood being
stripped away. It is not when everything is going well. It is in the
lean time when all you had hoped for seems to have hit a brick
wall, when no door you push seems to open and all around
seems as cold as the tundra and the heavens appear as brass. This
is when the Father, who loves His children so dearly, comes
with His ever-so-sharp secateurs, snip, snip, snipping away at our
outstretched fruitless arms, leaving us emaciated, isolated and

exposed in our weakness. This is pruning. It hurts to give up what we want to keep. Then He takes what remains of our once proud growth and bends it horribly where we do not want it to go, to train and bind us in crucifixion on the wires. Mature vines do not bend easily. They are quite rigid and flex only as hands and thumbs work along their length to crack and crush until the cane becomes flexible and bows to the pressure to be bent to the horizontal. This is how He deals with our self-life. It hurts to give up. How we dislike the training. How we complain at the bending and bowing. How our strength is broken as we finally succumb to the crucifixion!

Yet this is the time to rejoice! If only we could understand the reasoning of God. If only we truly believed we would know that the Father is treating us as sons and daughters and that from this season of pain and cutting would come growth and fruit in abundance. For if the vine were not so trained, fruiting would eventually give way to the endless production of wood, a wood fit only for the fire. We must learn to go through God's process with rejoicing, knowing that for every winter a spring will follow, and that for every pruning a fruiting will come.

How often have we read the passage in John 15 that tells us the Father is the One who prunes us so that we will produce fruit? Pruning equals fruit. Fruiting means there has been pruning. Every time the fruit bearing plant fruits it is cut back, it draws its strength from the parent plant to produce more fruit – it's a cycle that must be perpetuated. We must continually be forced back into relationship with the Father from whom we draw our strength and wisdom. Great is the folly of him who sees his fruit and thinks he now possesses the ability to produce fruit at will. No matter how hard he tries he will not succeed on his own. The only way to keep producing is to keep being pruned. It is a process that keeps us focused on the Lord. I believe that if we fully enter this process we will eventually become like the trees beside the river of God which fruit every month, not just once a year.

" . . . and on either side of the river, was the tree of life, which bore twelve fruits, each tree yielding its fruit every month. The leaves of the tree were for the healing of the nations."

(Revelation 22:2)

Time is not important to God in the way it is to us, but I do believe He encourages us towards frequency.

But our lovely Lord Jesus does not ask us to travel this road alone.

"For we do not have a High Priest who cannot sympathise with our weakness, but was in all points tempted [tested] *as we are, yet without sin"*

(Hebrews 4:15)

Our High Priest Jesus suffered a violent pruning on the cross. One might even say that on the cross He was planted in a grand prophetic gesture that underlined His right to claim He was the vine and that it was there that His blood (the fruit of the vine) was taken into the heavenly tabernacle where it rests forever in atoning sacrifice.

We read in John 15, that great passage of the Bible where Jesus tells us He is the vine, and we apply it to ourselves and try to work out what it means for us. I sometimes wonder what it must have meant for Jesus to talk in that way about Himself, knowing all that He knew of His life and death to come. And later, what a conflict must have raged within Him as He sought the Father's will in the Garden of Gethsemane.

"Father, if you are willing, take this cup from me; yet not my will, but yours be done."

(Luke 22:42 NIV)

This was the place where Jesus had to fully accept His humanity in all its stark reality. The place where God showed Him His need to drink from the cup of eternal salvation. The fullness of the Holy Spirit would avail nothing now; His communion with the Father would avail nothing. He would be planted on a hill, Jesus the vine, with His roots having to reach many metres down to the depths where His faith alone would assure Him He was who He said He was, and that He was doing the right thing according to the will of His Father.

Most vines are planted on stony ground. When rain penetrates the ground, it dissolves chemicals in the rocks and stones and these release gasses. These gasses in turn split the rocks, and the vine roots further exploit the cracks as they search deep down to find the nourishment they need. The hill Golgotha that Jesus was planted on was also rocky ground devoid of earth. No easy nourishment here for the vine Jesus. He too, would need to burrow deep, His roots searching in the dark places for that nugget of sustenance to maintain His Spirit.

Wood cut from the vine is of little value. Its main use is as a fuel for the fire, to be consumed. God often uses wood, or to be more precise trees, as another analogy for man.

"But blessed is the man who trusts in the LORD,
  whose confidence is in him.
He will be like a tree planted by the water."

(Jeremiah 17:7 NIV)

But where a tree is living, we talk of wood to indicate that the life of the tree is over. And wood is associated with sacrifice. The brazen altar in Moses' Tabernacle was made of wood overlaid with bronze, and wood was used to burn the sacrifice, even as Jesus was placed on the wood of the cross for His ultimate sacrifice. In the Tabernacle of Moses and the Temple of Solomon, the most holy place was lined with wood, not just on the floor but on the walls and the ceiling as well. This was overlaid with gold to show the glory of God covering the wood of sacrifice, willingly given up for the glory of God.

God loves our woody sacrifices, especially when they come from a pure heart. When we sacrifice to earn brownie points with Him, or to try to make Him do what we want, we simply create a smoke from our sacrifice, a smoke that is likely to become a stench in the nostrils of God. But the willing response to His touch becomes a sweet fragrant offering of love to our Lord and He Himself covers it with refiner's gold to reflect His glory. So we must submit to our vine wood being cut by our Father, from hearts that acknowledge His love and allow the wood to be felled joyously. Then the burning of our wood will indeed become a sweet fragrance to Him.

Chapter 8
Principles of Growth and Pruning for Harvest

Sometime in the middle of March as I walk under the thick brown stem of the vine on our pergola, I notice what appears to be raindrops on the patio beneath, arranged in a neat line. They are not raindrops of course, but the sap rising and oozing out from the end of each cut cane. An excitement grips me, because although I cannot see inside the plant, I know that the life of a new growing year has started again. From this tiny drop of sap I know that grapes are coming – as long as I imitate my Father and tend them as any good vinedresser – just like Adam and Noah. What is this sap?

Sap is how all plants grow. Sap is basically just water containing nutrients and minerals that have been extracted from the soil by the plant's roots. These elements are then transported through the plant by cells, known as xylem, all the way from the roots to the place where the growth will develop – the buds. At first it doesn't look as if very much is happening, but every drop of sap brings much needed building materials for growth. The rising of the sap is triggered by a number of catalysts, including the warmth of the sun and the lengthening hours of daylight. When all the conditions are just right the trigger is released and the process of growth begins.

I sometimes wonder why, in the Church, we allow disappointments to cloud our view of what is really happening in the spiritual realm. We watch the sap rising but don't really believe the fruiting process is in motion. The ultimate fruiting of the Church is that we so, *"Prepare the way of the* LORD*"* (Matthew 3:3), that He responds and says, "Here I come! I'm coming for my Bride! All is prepared!" But does our lack of faith block the path? How often do we observe outpourings of the Spirit, revivals, Toronto's, Brownsville's, Africa's and China's and wait for it to die down so we can continue as we were? Do we not understand that this is the sap of the Spirit rising, declaring to us that if we will only believe we will prepare the way for the coming of our Lord and He will come?

I have noticed over my more than two decades of personal salvation that we so often sit back and ask, "What next?" not realising this is a process to be involved with not merely observed. The rising of the sap in my vines causes me to watch for the bud burst, for the beginnings of growth. Why? Because my job is to tend those vines and care for them, so I'll be there for them as soon as they need me. I want to be there. I have to be there.

Sap rising should send a shiver of excitement through us all – God's on the move. Do we want to be left behind in the desert, or do we want to be where God leads us? Doctrine, hermeneutics, eschatology, denominations and anything else you can think of doesn't really come into it. The question the Church has to answer is only, "Do I want to be where God is?"

As it grows, delightful as it appears in its vigorous growth, the vine has very limited strength. All its energy is directed towards growing for the light. How many young Christians have you known like this? On fire for God and going to transform the world? As yet they have made no wood. They are all sap. Strengthening takes time. The vine, growing by transporting materials through its xylem cells, slowly strengthens the walls of the xylem to give them rigidity with a substance called lignin. Gradually the lignin transforms the cell into wood. The vine simply creates new xylem for the building work to continue. Only when enough wood has been created can the cane be handled with rougher hands. Until then, great care must be taken not to bend them and to give them extra support on wires or canes. Failure to understand this simple principle of nurture jeopardises the vine and thus its potential harvest. The vine canes are extremely brittle in the early stages and snap off at the merest hint of pressure. Losing contact with the main stem of the vine, their leaves hang limp and lifeless within an hour.

I have seen similar pressure applied in well-meaning churches with the result that many brothers and sisters in Christ are lost in the early months because of a lack of understanding of the need for basic nurture. The vigorous growth of the vine comes not from those who nurture and tend it, but from the vine itself. What happens is that we are too slow to encourage new Christians to get their food from the sustainable source of Jesus, rather than from the pastoral staff, and sometimes the new Christian chooses the warmth of the pastoral staff over developing a relationship with Him, sadly, to their own detriment.

Growth of the new canes is allowed until they have developed about four feet. At this point the growing tip is pinched out and stopped. If this is not done the cane will not fruit. All its energy goes into new growth. If unchecked, this growth will continue all season and with some varieties can produce canes in excess of fifteen feet. Pretty impressive for one season's growth, but quite useless! The only thing to be done with it is to cut it off and burn it, or perhaps prune it hard and train it onto the wires for fruiting in the following year.

Our churches are overstocked with un-pruned, unstopped, immature wood. Christians who spend all their time learning, going to conferences, reading books, listening to tapes or watching the God channel. None of this is wrong in essence, in fact all these things are the "nutrients" we need for growth. But too much of them and we become long, stringy canes that wave about in the wind and get in everyone else's way.

We must allow the Lord to bring training and discipline to our growth so that the nutrients produce good fruit, not hot air! It is difficult because we are so enthusiastic about knowing more and more about our wonderful Lord that there are times when we can't seem to get enough teaching. We don't realise that learning about Him, exciting and relevant as that is, is not the same as knowing Him. Learning about Him is an activity of the brain. Knowing Him is altogether different – an event of the heart.

Our Father is a pruner. Ouch! I tend to want to go on absorbing more and more, even to the point that, when my growing tip is cut off, like the vine I try to branch out sideways from every place a leaf is developing. I'll jolly well grow somehow! But Father pruner will persist by pinching out those side shoots too until we get the message that He wants fruit not endless knowledge.

Sometimes we think that if someone talks about Jesus absolutely all the time, this must be fruit of the Holy Spirit. But in my experience, those who constantly spiritualise every sentence rarely have much fruit in their lives. They often have much knowledge and will tell you all about the latest work of God in Somewheresville. They will know exactly what the Rev. Theo Logist says about post-, pre- or anti-millennialism, and probably could send you an email with the tour dates of the latest Christian Road Show. All good stuff and very informative and I'm sure someone needs to know it. But how many people did they bring to Christ last year? Whose lives have been changed or set free by their ministry? How do they bless and serve their local body? Do they reflect the love and character of Jesus? That's the real fruit all the knowledge is supposed to produce in us, and in between those two positions is another one of God's little processes, which we can see at work in the vine.

Do you remember how the xylem cells carry the nutrients to the parts where the plant needs them? One of the things the plant builds is leaves. And now, from the leaves, a new cell called phloem carries sugars converted in the leaves by the action of sunlight, in suspension in the sap, back through the plant to the fruit. All those nutrients that could otherwise have become useless extra wood, now instead become the building blocks of fruit. And what changes the nutrients to sugars is exposure to the light of the sun.

What the knowledgeable but fruitless Christian does not do is allow the light of Jesus to penetrate and transform the knowledge he has in his head to become revelation knowledge in his heart. This is where we must know Jesus. It is only from changed hearts that we will affect others by giving them fruit with the seed in it to produce a harvest in their hearts in turn.

Once, I had been through a very dark and lonely time as a young Christian. I had just joined a new church after six months of wandering and wondering, and my new home group leader suggested that next week we should go around the room and tell of all the good things God had done in our lives recently. "That won't take long then!" I murmured ungraciously beneath my breath. Next week came and I still had nothing to say. Life had been awful. I had lost all my friends, I was living alone in a one room bed-sit, I was hard up, work was difficult, and I did not know where God was in my life. They began testimonies on my left and worked away from me round the circle. By the time they got to the chap next to me, I was sweating about what I would say. I had nothing. The home group leader turned to me and invited me to speak. Just at that moment God did something quite extraordinary and very suddenly as He sometimes does! I had always wondered if there would come a time in my walk as a Christian where I would wander away from God. I used to look at some of these older saints who had been with Him for ten, twenty or thirty years and wonder if I would have the strength to make it that far. I was frightened that I might lose Him. But just as I was about to speak, He moved the scripture that says *"Christ in you, the hope of glory"* (Colossians 1:27) from my head to my heart. Suddenly, as He shone revelation light on the scripture, I understood! It wasn't up to me to make sure we stayed in touch! It was up to Him because He had taken up residence in me! And He says that He will never leave me or let me go! It is not about me hanging on to Him. And then, of course, I saw that this was what

He had been teaching me for the last six months. Here I was, still seeking after Him, because He is alive in me and His Holy Spirit in me always wants to seek Him! Fantastic! Now, when I counsel someone in similar straits, I have a spiritual authority, a true revelation knowledge or understanding in my heart to encourage them with, not just a head knowledge of the Scripture.

Unfortunately, many of us do not understand that these changes come as we submit ourselves to the pruning shears of God, and that is always uncomfortable. Neither do we understand that God sometimes prunes by using other people, as well as doing it sovereignly Himself. But we squirm and wriggle out of the shears when someone in authority in the church suggests a course of action (or inaction), saying that God is our only guide. What a deception that is. God is in the process of building the Church into a mighty army and I have yet to see a successful army that has no structure of authority. God never takes away our free will – we can choose to submit to authority or not. But persistent refusal ends up as mutiny and puts us in a place of rebellion against God, which is not wise. Submission to one another is God's safe place for us all, leaders and followers alike.

One reason we get in a mess with all this is that not only do we not want to submit to leadership, but leaders don't often understand how to pastor this growth. We seem to see it as acceptable, even commendable, for enthusiasm to run riot. No wonder God says that,

> *"Many shepherds [pastors] will ruin my vineyard*
> *and trample down my field;*
> *they will turn my pleasant field*
> *into a desolate wasteland."*
>
> (Jeremiah 12:10 NIV)

Effective pastoral work has backbone to it, yet we often seem so intent on trying to please everyone, or at least not upset them, that we probably deserve the title Evangellyfish!

In the early years of our church, three of us went away for a leader's weekend of teaching and encouragement. How well I remember Roger Davin giving twelve useful pointers for leaders. It was our first exposure to any form of leadership training although we had been leading a small group for a couple of years. We were pleasantly encouraged by the first seven headings. We were not at the top of the class, but we had been making the right kind of progress according to a man who had been there and was doing it. But then came the bombshell. "Your ability to say 'Yes' must be matched by an equal and opposite ability to say 'No'". We looked at each other in horror. We only ever said, "Yes". None of us could remember ever having said, "No" to anyone! We had certainly wanted to, but had somehow never thought we could, especially if it would upset them. Then we would be responsible for them being upset! But that's actually their responsibility, not ours, and in any case, there were those who knew how to manipulate circumstances to their advantage and our expense! The balance is that our ability to say, "No" actually gives much more credibility to when we say, "Yes". The power to speak into people's lives is greater because we can say both. Now people can hear it when we say, "No". The more we understand this and walk in it, the more lives will be transformed into the likeness of Jesus, who was very balanced in this regard.

Some years ago, a girl in the church had been sleeping with her boyfriend and become pregnant. We counselled the man, who had some serious issues, for some weeks about the need for marriage. We were straightforward with him and lovingly explained the counsel of Scripture. He submitted to the "pruning" and they were eventually married. They now have two children and are a real asset to the church and a credit to Jesus. The man testified after our counsel that we were the first people in his life to ever tell him he was way out of line, make him aware of the consequences, and urge him to sort things out one way or the other.

In the age we live in, many children are brought up without fathers or with dysfunctional parents who have themselves missed out on proper parenting. It is part of the job of Church leadership or eldership to provide proper fathering, which includes discipline, and we as children must learn to love being fathered, including the discipline!

Any parent, who has learned to include loving discipline in their skills will tell you that children like discipline and will sometimes even "ask" for it subconsciously by presenting unacceptable behaviour that forces parents to bring correction. Afterwards the child is noticed to be relaxed and cheerful. Why is this? Because the discipline has confined the child to boundaries within which he/she feels safe. Now they no longer have to face the challenges and responsibilities their unchecked activities were drawing them towards, and for which they felt totally ill-equipped. Christians are no different. We all draw comfort from the older more mature ones directing and correcting us.

> *"Blessed be the God and Father of our Lord Jesus Christ, the Father of mercies and God of all comfort, who comforts us in all our tribulation, that we may be able to comfort those who are in any trouble, with the comfort which we ourselves are comforted by God."*
>
> (2 Corinthians 1:3–4)

Sometimes the vinedresser goes a step further with his pruning and actually reduces the amount of fruit a branch or vine can carry. This regulates the vine to a quantity of grapes that is sustainable in subsequent years. If every bunch is allowed to ripen, too much energy can be sucked from the plant and the following years will be spent in recovery before normal production can be resumed. We should not fear this pruning. Father knows what we can sustain and does not want us barren because we've tried to produce too much all at once. How many people do you know of who have "burned out" because they would not let God prune away a bit of excess fruit?

Often this same pruning of potential bunches is done with the specific aim of reducing quantity in favour of quality. The resultant juice and wine is therefore of a higher quality than would have been the case were the vine allowed to crop all it wanted to. Our Father does exactly the same.

> *"...every branch that bears fruit He prunes, that it may bear more fruit."*

(John 15:2)

The Father is after quality, not just quantity. I don't know about you, but I don't much like it when my "quantity" is reduced, but I confess that I love great quality. Dear brothers and sisters, we must learn to love quality in the Church rather than quantity. Quantity brings more problems than it is sometimes worth and can even stifle that which could have been good. But quality is worth its weight in gold every time!

The vine always has what has just fruited cut away because the vinedresser knows that the old wood that bore fruit will never do so again. In cutting the old away, the vinedresser is encouraging the vine to put all its energy and strength towards the new growth that will produce more fruit. We object to this pruning because we dislike losing something that we think is of value to us and it can be momentarily painful. But God never prunes away anything that is useful to us, only that which is now useless, for to keep the useless would prevent us from developing new fruit, just as the vine, left with old fruit on its branches, will ramble aimlessly and produce nothing.

In the great vineyards of France, the vines are pruned both in the late autumn and early spring, and each time the vines are cut they weep at the wounds for twenty days and nights before the wound is healed. Twice twenty is forty. Can you grasp the depth of this picture? Our Lord Jesus, our Vine, weeps for forty days and nights every year. What does He weep for if not for His Church and the lost, that which has lost contact with Him, that which has been pruned away? Yet His tears are not only of sorrow but of joy too, for He knows the harvest is coming for it was Him who wrote

> *"Those who sow in tears*
> *Shall reap in joy."*
>
> (Psalm 126:5)

God uses prunings to expose our shortcomings. That which rises up in opposition to the pruning is the very thing that prevents the fruit coming. It has to be cut away. I once played in a worship band, and felt the Lord wanted me to play prophetically. But I didn't want to submit to the worship leader when he said "Not yet". I felt he didn't understand what was happening and had missed the moment. I was upset and had my nose put out of joint, so I complained to God. But God spoke sternly to me and told me to submit to his authority as worship leader. I needed pruning to sit under his authority as worship leader and allow some humility to grow. Ten minutes later, the worship leader invited me to bring what I felt I had. Needless to say, God moved powerfully, as He always will when we are obedient to Him.

Have you noticed, pruning happens year after year? No pruning this year means no fruit next year. There simply is no escaping the cut if we want fruit. God always wants fruit so He will always offer the cut, year after year. He never allows us to bypass the cut and go another way. He never says, "Oh all right then, you can have some fruit this year and then we'll try pruning again next year." No, He says the only way is the cut, otherwise, no fruit.

Perhaps we should look again at the parable of the fig tree.

> *"And seeing a fig tree by the road, He came to it and found nothing*
> *on it but leaves, and said to it, 'Let no fruit grow on you ever*
> *again.' Immediately the fig tree withered away."*
>
> (Matthew 21:19)

Jesus cursed the tree because it was not doing what it was designed to do. God made all the trees on the third day of creation and they were made to bear fruit with the seed in itself.

> *"Then God said, 'Let the earth bring forth grass, the herb that yields seed, and the fruit tree that yields fruit according to its kind, whose seed is in itself, on the earth;' and it was so."*
>
> (Genesis 1:11)

Fruit trees that do not bear fruit are of no use. It is only as they are properly cared for and respond to good nurture that fruit comes. How fortunate for us that the balance of Scripture suggests that Jesus is the God of the "one more" chance, but how short-sighted of us if we continually ignore His purpose and resist His cuts.

Chapter 9

Harvest Time

Harvest time is so important. I have struggled for more than ten years to produce a good grape harvest and a wine worthy of being drunk. After nine years I finally made a few bottles of wine I am not too ashamed of! And it's not just the harvest, but the quality of the grapes, and this is based on the amount of natural sugar or sweetness in them. There's a lesson for us Christians in this. I wonder how many of us would pass the sweetness test? Below a certain level of natural sweetness it really is not worth the trouble of trying to make wine.

We began our vineyard in 1993 with nearly fifty vines. I remember planting them with my three-year-old daughter Sarah. We prayed over every single one and commanded them in the name of Jesus to be fruitful. By the time 1995 came we were really excited and eager to see the first grapes. And grapes we saw, even with half a crop, enough to make some five gallons of juice.

It had been a constructive year for us in the garden. We had roofed between two outbuildings on the back of the house and made a small conservatory, laid a cream coloured patio right across the back of the house and then added brick planters and a pergola. Another small lean-to had been kitted out so we had somewhere to make the wine. In due time we harvested, the juice was pressed, the yeast added for the fermentation and the whole transferred to a five gallon glass jar. It was late on Saturday night, everyone else had gone to bed and I couldn't resist just one more look at the wine bubbling away through its airlock, before I too went to bed.

That's when I noticed the wine was frothing up right through the airlock and spilling onto the shelf. There was nothing for it, late though it was, except to transfer some of the wine to another overspill jar until the ferment was less volatile. That's when it happened. Disaster struck. As I lifted the heavy jar with one hand underneath and the other around the neck for support, the whole neck and six inches of the top of the jar cracked off in my hand. It was one of those moments when time seemed almost to stand still. In an elongated split-second I knew that I would not be able to hold the jar and the five gallons in one hand, that it was going to drop, that my three year wait for harvest would be deferred another whole year; that I would very upset about that and that there was absolutely no point in being upset about it, so I may as well not be! All of that and still I had time to watch as the jar fell in slow motion onto the stone steps that led from the kitchen to the lean-to.

The jar smashed into a thousand pieces and the wine splashed down both sides of the lean-to which has a gentle slope to the door to the patio. The door was still open to the autumn night. Reaching the corners of the lean-to, the wine was diverted towards the open door where both streams met in a mini tidal wave, which then gushed out of the back door and ran in a blood red river across the new cream patio. The harvest was lost – there was simply nothing I could do except watch. I didn't know whether to cry, kick myself or the cat (if we had one) or be philosophically stoic! I settled in my immature way for angrily asking God "Why?" And He answered, as He sometimes does, with a clarity that is both instant and crystal clear, leaving you in no doubt that it is Him. I was watching the red trail on the patio disappear into the dark of the night as He said, "So you would understand something of the pain in My heart when my Son's blood was spilt on the ground and nobody took any notice."

I was shocked and ashamed that my self-righteous anger could so blindly centre me on myself. I had not really stopped to think what it must have felt like for the Father when Jesus was sacrificed for us. Many times I had thought of Jesus on the cross, but never the Father watching. What a conflict of emotions there must have been. He could have rescued Jesus at any time, and indeed Jesus could have called on legions of angels to come to His aid, but chose not to. Here was the Father's own Son being sacrificed before His very eyes, yet He could not intervene if His great purpose of redemption was to be accomplished. Jesus' blood had to be spilled for the greater joy of redeeming mankind. The nearest I get to it is trying to understand David's emotions as he wept for his son who was also hung on a tree (by his hair) and whose side was also pierced by a spear.

> *"O my son Absalom – my son, my son Absalom – if only I had died in your place! O Absalom my son, my son!"*
>
> (2 Samuel 18:33)

How often do we need reminding what it cost to shed the blood of Jesus? God needed to remind me that night.

But God wasn't finished talking about the spilled wine just yet. The next morning we were in the midst of morning worship when a lady with a prophetic ministry in our church spoke out a word from the Lord. Our church, like many others, was in the early days of hearing about the wonderful outpouring of God's Spirit in Toronto. Some had already been to Toronto and others were planning trips. This lady knew nothing of the events of the previous night at my house, but she said, "In the house of the prophet, a sign. Of this new wine of My Spirit which is being poured out on the earth, there is no container built that can hold it in!"

In our fellowship I am recognised as a prophet and she was speaking about wine poured out on the earth in the house of a prophet! I was overwhelmed. God had set the whole thing up! Well if that's what it costs to know that His Spirit is never going to be bottled up again, that's fine by me. It sounds pretty much like the prophecy of Joel happening in our time.

> *"And it shall come to pass afterward*
> *That I will pour out My Spirit on all flesh . . .*
> *And it shall come to pass*
> *That whoever calls on the Name of the LORD*
> *Shall be saved."*
>
> (Joel 2:28, 32)

Do you see how that scripture is linked to the final harvest? The time is upon us. Harvest is fun. Harvest is what it's all about. If there is no harvest, why do we do church?

I'll never forget that first harvest coming. Every morning I could hardly wait to get down to the vines and see how the bunches of grapes were coming on. It was magical to watch them over time, gradually swelling and then turning from a pale translucent green to a rich deep purple with a slightly blue tinge. I kept saying "well done" and "keep going, you're almost ready for harvest" to them. I made sure that every leaf was in place and that all the grapes were safe and secure from the unwanted attentions of birds! They became like children to me. I petted and cosseted them and as I did so, I used to think of the Lord doing the same with us, His vineyard, His children. I thought of how thrilled He must be when He sees our harvest appearing; of how He loves to encourage us and lead the cheering of the vast cloud of witnesses that surrounds us!

> *"In that day sing to her,*
> *'A vineyard of red wine!*
> *I, the LORD, keep it,*
> *I water it every moment;*
> *Lest any hurt it,*
> *I keep it night and day.'"*
>
> (Isaiah 27:2–3)

God looks after His Church and tends it. Unfortunately harvest does not always come because we fail to allow God to do His work in our lives, often substituting our own ideas instead of His – the old problem back in the Garden of Eden. I don't mean to suggest for a moment that that's how it is in your church, but it happens in some. May God give us the grace to tend our vineyards as His co-workers unto harvest, not as those who trample underfoot.

> *"For we are God's fellow workers."*
>
> (1 Corinthians 3:9)

We work with God, not on our own. That way we end up doing what He wants done, not producing something on our own and hoping He will like it. That would put us back in the place of earning conditional love. His love is not conditional. Part of God's judgement on Israel was for precisely this problem. They had not included God in their life equation and instead sought to make their own harvest.

> *"Israel empties his vine,*
> *He brings forth fruit for himself."*
>
> (Hosea 10:1)

Or, in the words of the most sung commercial song in history, "I did it my way." No, the Lord is building a relationship with us that will last for eternity and it is only out of that relationship that true harvest will come. It's His vineyard, He is the Vinedresser and He will determine when the harvest is ready.

In the beautiful little French wine town of St Emillion, a body of viticulture professionals known as the *Jurade*, proclaim the start of the harvest from the top of the King's Tower. Harvest is not a random event. Its timing is crucial and getting it right is the job of those who are in a position to judge ripeness. Our King will

make a similar proclamation through one of His angels when the
time is right for our harvest.

> *"And another angel came out from the altar, who had power over*
> *fire, and he cried with a loud cry to him who had the sickle,*
> *saying, 'Thrust in your sharp sickle and gather the clusters of the*
> *vine of the earth, for her grapes are fully ripe.' So the angel thrust*
> *his sickle into the earth and gathered the vine of the earth, and*
> *threw it into the great winepress of the wrath of God. And the*
> *winepress was trampled outside the city, and blood came out of*
> *the winepress, up to the horses' bridles, for one thousand six*
> *hundred furlongs."*
>
> (Revelation 14:18–20)

I don't know if you realise quite how big that wine lake will be. It
will certainly beat anything the EU can store up! One thousand six
hundred furlongs is two hundred miles, which means the lake will
be about four hundred miles across, to a depth of perhaps six feet.
I am no mathematician, but my rough calculations make that
around thirteen billion bottles of wine. That's much more wine
than there are people in the world. God likes to deal with excess.
When the spies went into the Promised Land ahead of the
Israelites, they came back from the valley of Eshcol carrying a
bunch of grapes between two men on a pole (Numbers 13:23).
That must have been some bunch of grapes! I wish I could get my
vines to crop like that. But these are the kind of measures God
uses and believe it or not, that is the measure of the harvest that is
coming to the Church. You and I have never seen anything like it
before.

Chapter 10

Harvest Festival and Communion

If all of our Christian rituals and traditions were done away with bar one, the one most of us would surely want to keep would be Communion. Of everything that we do, it alone brings us close to the One whom we love and serve and through it alone, does He speak with such tenderness, love and compassion, reminding us over and over of His payment for our sin and of His forgiveness for us. In John 6, Jesus spoke to the Jews in the synagogue at Capernaum. He told them that He was the bread of life come down from heaven (v. 51) and that unless we ate His flesh and drank His blood we would not have eternal life. Later in John 17:3 He tells us that eternal life is about knowing "the Father, the only true God and Jesus Christ whom He has sent." Put together, what these two scriptures mean, is that if we know the Father and Jesus, we will want to remember Him in communion. This is what He established when He passed the bread and the cup at the last supper.

> *"This is my blood of the new covenant, which is shed for many for the remission of sins."*

(Matthew 26:28)

Except, of course, that He substituted wine for blood. The use of wine was not a whim of Jesus'. It could have been juice or milk or water. He chose wine, and *oinos* – the Greek word meaning alcoholic wine at that. Jesus knew He was God's vine and as such, blood and wine were interchangeable to Him. Wine is the fruit of vineyards and God was again drawing our attention to the fact that He planted a vineyard because He wanted some wine at the end of it.

This idea of communion being representative of the work of Jesus was not new. It had been in the heart of God for a long time. The first time vines themselves are talked about in the Bible is in part of the story of Joseph. Joseph had been sold into captivity in Egypt where he had fallen foul of his master and ended up in jail. Whilst there, two of his fellow inmates had dreams and they came to Joseph to see if he could interpret them. The butler or cupbearer, saw a vine with three branches. The vine was laden with fruit, which he took, pressed into Pharaoh's cup and gave to him to drink. The interpretation was clear. The three branches were three days, and in that time he would be restored to his position at the right hand of Pharaoh. This was great news for the butler and it happened just as Joseph said.

But God was doing much more than just telling us how he restored the butler. It is a picture of communion. It is also a picture of resurrection, another "third day" story, a picture that foresees the blood of the risen Lord Jesus atoning for us and giving us life. The butler was forgiven for whatever his crime was, his sentence wiped out and his prison clothes removed in exchange for acceptable attire. He was cleansed, just as we are by the blood of Christ, and he was restored to his position at the right hand of Pharaoh, even as we are seated with Christ in heavenly places (Ephesians 2:6).

The baker, on the other hand saw three baskets of bread on his head, which the birds of the air devoured. For him the interpretation was death in three days' time. The poor baker was duly executed. Here again is a picture and type of communion. Jesus said that the bread represented His body that was broken for us. In this story the birds of the air ate the bread. Here the judgement of God is on the humanity of Jesus for the sins of the world. His body broken for us. No wonder the poor baker would have to die, how could he take that on his shoulders? Yet as much as the baker would have to die, the butler would have to live, because in the dream he received wine from the eternal vine, Jesus. Since the Word of God says that "the life is in the blood" (Genesis 9:4) and Jesus declared that "the wine is my blood", that is what the butler received – life.

Even before Joseph interpreted those two dreams, Jesus had staked a claim in Scripture to bread and wine. It's a strange little story that begins in Genesis 14:18 and relates how Abram, returning from rescuing his nephew Lot from four marauding kings, was met by an odd character called Melchizedek, who brought out bread and wine which he offered to him. At first glance this could look like it was just a nice gesture by Melchizedek, seeking to refresh someone who had been up all night chasing bandits and rescuing a friend, but closer examination reveals that something quite extraordinary was being acted out by God.

Melchizedek is described as not only the king of Salem but also the priest of God Most High. There is no doubt in my mind that this is what is called a theophany, an appearance of Jesus in the Old Testament. There are other examples, as when He appeared to Joshua as Commander of the Armies of the Lord, but this one is particularly important. "Salem" means peace, so this man was the "king of peace". Isaiah 9:6 says that the saviour, Jesus, will be the Prince of Peace. Later, the writer to the Hebrews confirms this when he further says of Melchizedek that He was the,

> " 'king of righteousness' ... without father, without mother, without genealogy, having neither beginning of days nor end of life, but made like the Son of God ... "
>
> (Hebrews 7:2–3)

Only one person fits that bill, Jesus. There is no other person who is remotely able to claim such titles.

So here is Jesus appearing in the Old Testament and He's offering bread and wine to Abram. Jesus, the Alpha and Omega, beginning the process of redemption by offering the redemptive symbols of His own body and blood to the very man who was about to become the father of many nations, the Church, who would all need that redemption! It's a "first the physical, then the spiritual" communion story being offered to the Church through the body of Abram, before the actual and spiritual offering of Jesus' body and blood for the Church on the cross. Jesus the Alpha and Omega, taking the Omega to the Alpha! Taking the completion of His work to the man chosen to father His work! Bringing the father of what would become the Church, both Jews and gentiles, the elements of the sacrificial gift, which will eventually unite and fulfil the destiny of the Church as the Bride of Christ! Jesus the everlasting offers Abram of the Old Covenant His body and blood of the New Covenant and blesses Him. No wonder then that over the course of the next three chapters, Abram was given the everlasting covenant by the Father, sealed with the exchange of names whereby Abram would now take on the "h" sound of the name of God and become Abraham, and God would change His name from "I AM" to "I AM, THE GOD OF ABRAHAM". What an amazing event! What an amazing God!

The Word of God speaks great mysteries at times. Paul declared that, Abraham is *"the father of all those who believe"* (Romans 4:11).

Aren't you glad that when you were "in the loins of Abraham" Jesus came to offer you His body and blood for redemption and to bless you with the everlasting kindness of God?

> *"But the mercy of the LORD is from everlasting to everlasting*
> *On those who fear Him,*
> *And His righteousness to children's children,*
> *To such as keep His covenant,*
> *And to those who remember His commandments to do them."*
>
> (Psalm 103:17–18)

Surely His commandments are easy in light of this promise. All we have to do is love God and love one another (Matthew 27) and all the blessings of God are upon us. This is why communion is such an important ritual for us to remember to keep. The problem is that we have made what was a celebration into a solemn ritual affair that rather misses the point and confines us to an arena that is not the whole counsel of God.

Recently Janice and I had an experience of communion which took us very much by surprise, which in itself was God backfiring on us our joke on our daughter! We had surprised our daughter Sarah with a week long holiday in the south of France. We had missed out on our usual summer holiday, but felt it right to go in the October half-term break. Sarah had stayed overnight with friends so we could secretly make the preparations in her absence. We packed the car and met her the next day at a wedding (no they didn't run out of wine!). Eventually we made our excuses and left the wedding to go home, but suggested we went for a drive first. Sarah was so busy chatting away that she didn't really notice we had driven all the way to Dover, and it was only as I showed our passports and confirmed our lane number and departure time that she realised what was happening. Success was ours, the surprise complete! We drove all night through the heart of France, stopping for a few hours' sleep in the car and breakfast, eventually arriving at the little seaside town of Banyuls-sur-mer in the afternoon.

Banyuls is in the bottom left-hand corner of France surrounded by the Pyrenees, which fall into the Mediterranean on both sides. Steep terraced vineyards cover the hillsides. It's part of the wine area known as Côtes du Roussillon. There was not a cloud in the sky and the temperature was in the high seventies as we rounded the final bend to look down on the beach and the town. There was a huge party going on in full swing! It was the annual Fête des Vendanges, the Grape Harvest Festival. To celebrate, the main street and the town square were festooned with brightly coloured balloons. Great clusters of purple "balloon" grapes hung from lamp-posts, and twisted strings of Catalan yellow and red hung across the road. It seemed like the whole town had come out onto the beach and the promenade. Tables were set on the beach and people had been feasting on great barbecues of pork and mussels. But at the centre of the feasting was bread – big chunky three foot long, ten inch wide loaves of fresh, warm, home-baked bread – and limitless quantities of the heady local red wine.

It wasn't long before we began to join in the fun. Being a musician, having first equipped myself with a gargantuan barbe-cued pork doorstep and a cup of red wine, I quickly gravitated to the nearest band. They looked very French! They wore stripy blue and white T-shirts and blue berets with white and red kerchiefs knotted around their necks. There were saxophones, trumpets, a clarinet, trombones, a euphonium and an accordion, a full drum kit, a separate bass drum and a bongo player who played with beaters – loudly! On the beach sprawled an exhausted sousaphone player! They played with enormous enthusiasm for which their lack of musicianship was regrettably not made up! It was difficult to know who was the one who was in tune so everyone seemed to make up their own mind as to what was correct. Starting was also a problem. Usually the lead trumpet player would shout out the name of the tune and then start on his own, the others coming in rather like a goods train clattering into motion. On more complex arrangements, after much loud debate, one would be chosen as conductor for the piece. He would then jab a finger in the direction of the lead trumpet player, who would begin as before, the rest following in the same manner. Either way, the effect was the same! However, they were having fun, and more to the point, so was everyone else – waltzing happily on the promenade, singing and smiling a great deal. It was a moment of life so good I wished I could capture it for ever, and I was laughing so much I could hardly eat my doorstep!

It was around this point that God did a "gotcha" on us who had earlier "got" our daughter. Right in the middle of all this fun He inconveniently began to talk about communion. I was surprised at first, because as far as I know, the people of Banyuls are no more or less godly or ungodly than people elsewhere, so how was it they were being used by God to talk of communion?

Gradually He began to explain. The people of Banyuls were celebrating their year's work and investment. In Banyuls you either work in tourism, a service industry, or vineyards. Someone in your family will most likely work with the vines or sell the produce or encourage outsiders to come and see what they do and sell. Daily they climb the steep-sided terraces to tend the vines, watching to ward off any disease as soon as it appears, or better, spraying with insecticides to prevent infections happening at all; training the vines and pruning them in the hot summer months to make sure as much energy goes into the crop as possible. Then there is the backbreaking work of pruning during the winter months and the constant replanting of new vines and "grubbing up" of the old. This is followed by the frantic work of harvest and the work of making, maturing and bottling. They have a huge personal investment in the vineyards so that when harvest comes they know the effort that went into making it successful and they know what they're celebrating.

I sometimes wonder if that is true in the Church. There are times when church can seem more like a cross between a spectator sport, a theatre, and a morgue! You know exactly what I mean. "Don't miss next Sunday. We've got the Amazing Preacher X coming all the way from Somewheresville and he is so funny." (That will keep us amused and happy for a week.) "And then at the end of the month the fantastic XYZ travelling dance and drama troupe (sorry, ministry!) will be with us!" (That should keep us all talking for a week!) OK, maybe that's a cynical view and you're not at all encouraged to go to your church for those kinds of reasons, but I'll bet you know some churches that are like that. I'm not saying that it's wrong for people to be entertaining when they speak, or that dance and drama have no place in the Church; far from it. But it becomes a problem when leaders seek to keep people happy rather than being more aware of what God wants to bring to His people, or when church-goers judge churches on how well they keep people entertained rather than how responsive they are to God.

Many of our churches are filled with apathetic folk who do not really get involved with the growth and work of the church. 80% of most church work is done by only 20% of the people. 80% of congregations do very little towards the life and work of the church. The outcome is little or no harvest and little to celebrate when we share the Lord's Supper. So we suddenly become very religious, introverted and reverentially hushed; we "internalise" and personalise and take deep breaths and adopt "holy" frowns! You know it's true, and yes, of course, there are times when all of that is acceptable. But all the time? Where's the remembrance that God doesn't remember me any more as a sinner, as someone who made a mess of life, who's promised everlasting mercy and peace to my children's children, who's love is excruciatingly wonderful, who will never leave me or forsake me, who satisfies the desires of my heart, who has prepared a mansion for me, who gives me His Holy Spirit for free, who comforts me and counsels me, who leads and guides me, who wants me to know Him as much as He knows me, who adopts me as His son and provides for all my needs, who gives me dignity, destiny, purpose, harvest and victory?!

I believe the Lord showed us that the people of Banyuls had tapped into the benefits of the vineyard and were celebrating because they understood what it cost. Happily it was a free celebration and anyone could join in just as we had done, but it had nowhere near the same meaning for us as it did for them. We had fun but didn't understand the full meaning. True communion is a celebration.

The strange band played its part too. Although musically lacking in many quarters, the one thing they excelled in was the generosity of spirit with which they performed. Over the last two decades I have watched with interest as the overall standard of musicianship within the church has improved. Some churches now present a professional quality of music and the pursuit of excellence in church will get my vote every time. All too often the Church allows a level of musicianship that is too painful for words with the excuse that "they're only doing it for the Lord". I feel led to say that the Lord is far more tolerant than most of us! There is a world of difference between doing something for the Lord in private and doing something for the Lord in public. Playing in public places a greater demand on musicians. In private we can play as badly as a first year student and our Father will listen attentively and applaud and encourage at the end. But His encouragement is to get us good enough to play in front of others.

Any parent with a musical child knows what I'm talking about. It's great when little Jack or Jill plays for you even if it is hard on the ears, but you want them to practise so that when they play for your friends or on stage, they play well and don't make everyone groan on the inside whilst smiling through gritted teeth. Professionalism and skill in the Church is the right direction to be travelling in, but useless in the Church and to the Lord without spirit and truth. Sometimes we can take the pursuit of excellence so far that we neglect the simple truth that worship music is primarily there to bless our Father in heaven and He will be thrilled with standards we sometimes find hard to accept. But He will ever be encouraging to bring us to better levels of skill. Whatever you do, do it as unto the Lord, a scripture underlined by the parable of the talents.

There is a saying that "balance is the ability to embrace all relevant extremes". If then, we pursue excellence at the expense of embracing the raw unrefined spirit, we have become imbalanced. Professionalism and skill alone are not the standards of the Church. Our standards are spirit and truth which are better expressed the greater our professionalism and skill. The band at Banyuls was a great reminder of these principles.

When the world is able to see the Church celebrate the enormous gift of God expressed with true thanksgiving, then all men will be drawn to Jesus, not to charismatic leaders or our entertaining services or to our great musicians, but to Jesus.

Chapter 11

Wine or Juice?

The reason for growing vines at all is to produce grapes. Some of these are eaten, providing a delicious fruit, sweet, soft and pleasant to the palette. So pleasant they're hard to resist when you're in a vineyard. God even says that you can eat your fill when you are in someone else's vineyard, but make sure you don't take any home with you!

> *"When you come into your neighbour's vineyard, you may eat your fill of grapes at your pleasure, but you shall not put any in your container."*
>
> (Deuteronomy 23:24)

A problem for biblical viticulturalists was what to do with all those fresh grapes ripening at about the same time. Fresh, soft fruit doesn't keep for long at the best of times, and 2,000 or 3,000 years ago there was little knowledge of food preservation, so the fresh produce of the vine, either fruit or juice, had to be consumed close to the growing season or preserved in the only ways they knew how. One way was to dry the grapes in the sun, a practice that is still carried out today. Dried red grapes are known as raisins and white grapes as sultanas.

The only real way of preserving the juice was to ferment it into wine, the alcohol acting as a preservative. Still today, the vast majority of grapes produced in the world are used to make wine.

Within the Church wine has created much controversy and produced some doctrines which quite frankly, are doctrines of demons, used by the devil to try to discredit the Church as unbalanced and over-religious. Because these views are passionately held by many, or commonplace within national boundaries, we tend to shy away from discussing them with any honesty. This is sad, because extreme views flourish where there is darkness. I do not believe my God works in darkness. Rather that is the domain of our enemy and the longer he can keep this subject in darkness, the longer he can manipulate it for his own ends. My God works in the light and says what He means.

"God is light and in Him is no darkness at all."

(1 John 1:5)

Extremists of the no drinking lobby suggest that the ancients didn't have wine in the way that we do – that it was only grape juice. But this is not borne out by Scripture. Grape juice is sometimes translated as "new wine" and I have heard it preached that this was non-alcoholic, however, this is not so. Even today, people drink new wine. Recently I visited the Czech Republic and my host suggested one night that we should drink *burcak* (pronounced "boo-shack"), or new wine. This wine is only available during a two-week period each year. The Bavarians drink it as *federweisser*. It is simply wine in the process of fermenting, hence it is cloudy and bubbly, both sweet from the unfermented juice and sour from the fermented part, but nonetheless alcoholic. Although it may not be as alcoholic as fully fermented wine, it is still quite heady and can easily catch one unawares. It was this new wine the disciples were suspected of having drunk too much of when they preached in Acts 2 filled with the Holy Spirit.

In the Old Testament "wine" means fermented grape juice 125 times out of the 150 it is referred to. The most common word in the Old Testament is *yayin*, which means "intoxicating wine as fermented". Noah got drunk and fell over on the same *yayin* that Melchizedek offered to Abram. The vine of Judges 9:13 would rather keep making the same *yayin* that gladdens the heart of both men and God. The New Testament only uses the word *oinos* and derivatives of it, with just the one reference to *glencos* or "new wine" (Acts 2) and both mean "intoxicating wine". Jesus produced over a thousand bottles of fabulous intoxicating *oinos* wine at the wedding feast in Cana. Most notably, He also called Himself a winebibber, (literally a tippler) describing Himself in stark contrast to John the Baptist who never touched a drop!

The Bible doesn't actually seem to mind if we drink wine or not. I know the subject of wine presents difficulties for many Christians and perhaps some would be happier if there were clear references in the Bible to the abstinence of alcohol for Christians, however none exists. What the Bible exhorts Christians to do is to have a healthy regard for the dangers of alcohol, warnings against excessive use, warnings against use that would offend another brother, and encouragement instead to drunkenness in the Spirit. Excess brings disrespect to God's temple, our bodies, and bondage. If we do drink wine, we should remain in control, not let it control us. A glass a day the older you get helps the heart remain healthy, but we must be aware that if someone else has a problem with drinking, we should abstain in his or her presence so as not to cause them to stumble. If someone chooses not to drink wine that is as much their choice as mine in exercising my freedom not to eat tripe and onions, because I don't happen to like it, and they should be respected in their view.

One of the reasons wine and other alcoholic drink is frowned upon in some circles of the Church is a legacy from the early days of those who sought to reach people who grew up with the effects of the industrial revolution and increasing urbanisation. William Booth and the Salvation Army were prominent in this arena and Booth's followers ministered particularly to sectors of the population that were rife with alcoholism. It was the nature of their ministry, amongst others, to rescue people from a dependence on alcohol, which gave rise to "taking the pledge" to abstain. It was never a command of Scripture, and valid though it was in context, we should not turn a perfectly legitimate old expediency into a modern doctrine unsupported in God's Word.

Wine is not evil in and of itself and does not need redemption. We are what needs redemption, along with our attitudes towards wine and those who drink it, and we need to be open to what God has to say about wine. Over the years I have discovered that God rarely if ever speaks in riddles. Secrecy is not His way. He is the light and He works and speaks in the light. He is clear and unambiguous. We are the ones who make things more complicated than they actually are. Some years ago our church received a prophetic word that we would be "the church in the marketplace". How we struggled with that. What could God mean? Were we to get involved with people in business, or with people in the finance world? Should we hold open-air meetings in the business areas of Croydon? What? Then one day, as we were sensing it was time for us to invest in a permanent building, someone told us of an old supermarket site that had been vacant for the last fourteen years in Surrey Street in Croydon. You've guessed? Surrey Street has hosted a daily market for the last nine hundred years! God meant exactly what He had said – we were to be the church in the "market place".

Planting a vineyard and growing grapes is half of God's story to us, the other half is making the wine and maturing it ready for drinking and this is a process that can take years. And it is all for a purpose – wine makes glad the heart of man and God (Judges 9:12–13). This "gladness" is where we often come unstuck. We are all well aware of the gladness that overtakes some with wine! We see it daily in the streets of our cities and we know the devastation that excess can and does cause to individuals and families. It is in the excess that the problems arise.

Our old friend Noah knew that excess. Strangely, after all he had been through, or maybe it was in that moment of success that his guard briefly came down, he took the wine of the vineyard he had planted, got drunk out of his mind and fell down naked on his bed. What a state to get into for this righteous man of God! He was so paralytic that having got his clothes off he fell over and passed out naked before he could get into bed! In Genesis 9:21 Ham, his son, saw his nakedness and instead of covering him up and saying nothing to anyone that would expose his father (as he should have done if he truly honoured him), he went off to have a laugh at his father's expense with his two brothers, Shem and Japheth. Our hearts are revealed by our actions. His brothers knew better than to undermine their father in such a way and instead of joining in with the joke, walked into Noah's bedroom backwards to cover his naked shame with a blanket.

This incident is interesting for the way it is recorded by the Holy Spirit. Ham is the one most rebuked for his behaviour in dishonouring his father, behaviour that earned him the curse of having to serve both of his brothers. The brothers are not singled out for mention or a pat on the back for their response. It's as if God expects righteous behaviour and doesn't reward us for doing what we are supposed to do. Then, of course, there is Noah. Is he rebuked for drunkenness? Is he rebuked for setting a bad example to his children? Is he rebuked for letting God down? No, none of these things are stacked against him. Perhaps when he woke the next morning with a rotten hangover, he remembered something of what had happened, at least that the empty wine skins had something to do with the way his head was feeling and that was enough for his heart to cry out to God in repentance. If so, that would have been sufficient for God to separate Noah from his sin as far as east is from west and remember it no more, and so it was never mentioned again. Would that we got our priorities right in church sometimes! At the very least, Noah would have been off most of our leadership teams and probably on a six-month compulsory counselling course, when perhaps all that had happened was that he had had a bad day, or just not realised how strong the wine was!

Jesus never distanced Himself from wine because He understood that there was more to it than merely being an alcoholic beverage – that it also held a prophetic quality. If Jesus is the vine and we are the branches (John 15) then we, the Church, are the part that is supposed to bear much fruit that will one day mature to become a wine that will gladden the hearts of many men with the life of Jesus. We are to become like Him, to put Him on daily, to be transformed into His likeness and to go and be His ambassadors throughout the world as we share the goodness of the gospel of peace. What else will so gladden the hearts of men?

Jesus' very first miracle was about just that. We should notice first that the story we know as the wedding feast at Cana is recorded as taking place on the third day. The Holy Spirit wants us to understand that the story we are about to read is significant because it deals with issues synonymous with resurrection and therefore, eternal life. This is another "third day" story, take note! God is talking to us about resurrection and the blood and life that will last for ever! This is a celebration story! It was near the end of the feast and they had run out of wine. We don't know exactly how many people were there, but anything over two hundred guests would make it a very rich wedding and extremely unlikely to run out of anything, most of all wine. We know the story in John 2. Jesus took six pots used for washing the guests' feet, had them filled to the brim with water and some of it poured out and taken to the master of the feast. The master did not know that it was washing pot water, although the servants did! I'll bet that was a great story to tell to their pals later. The master was astonished to find that it was some of the best wine he'd ever tasted and chided the bridegroom for keeping it back till late in the feast.

Each pot, we are told, held between 20 and 30 gallons. A gallon equals just over six standard 75cl bottles of wine. So Jesus produced between 720 and 1,080 bottles of top quality wine for maybe two hundred people who had already drunk plenty. That's perhaps four or five bottles for every man woman and child there! The word that comes to mind is "excessive". Yet evidently not to Jesus. He wanted everyone to know there was as much wine as anyone could possibly want for eternity. Enough of His blood to cleanse anyone who wanted it, enough to cleanse the deepest sin. There's enough to make your heart glad forever. That's why this is a third day story – it is speaking about the wonders of the finished work of Jesus that were ushered in with such triumph when He was resurrected and should give us such cause for celebration.

But there was more. Not only was this water from soiled jars turned into gladdening wine that amply covered the shame of the hosts running out, it was also fantastic wine. When you drink wine, the palette gradually becomes desensitised by the alcohol, so it's always wise to put out the best wine first and move on to the cheaper varieties later. That way your palette can appreciate the good wine before it is desensitised, and when it is, you can drink lesser quality wine without noticing the difference quite so much. But Jesus did the opposite to show that no gladdening of our hearts can compare with His. He alone has the wine to satisfy our hearts. Once we have drunk His wine there is no other better to come and all that has gone before is forgotten.

I really cannot see my Jesus sitting on the sidelines as all this was going on "tut tutting" at all the guests enjoying the effects of drinking the wine He had just made, taking notes for judgement day! I can't see Him refusing a cup Himself or having a laugh and a joke with the other guests, and I can see Him chuckling at Malachi and old Mrs Samuels dancing together, a little "in their cups". Quite apart from anything else it would have been a bit two-faced having just made a thousand bottles of the finest wine! Much of Jesus' popularity with the people was due to the fact that He was accessible. He wasn't on another planet like the Pharisees, always striving to be more holy and religious than anyone else, setting themselves apart from the people, allowing them admission only if they crossed over and became like them. Jesus was always with the people where they were, doing what they did. You could reach out and touch Him or ask Him questions. He never condemned or pushed away. The people saw His godliness, but they also saw His humanity. Jesus rebuked the Pharisees (Luke 7:31–35) for exactly the attitude that had kept the people at arms' length from them and for the religious way they had judged Jesus. In effect He said to them, "You've offered the people a form of godliness and complained because they haven't taken up your offer. That's because you don't know that godliness comes from knowing God, it's not related to behaviour alone. You thought that John the Baptist was demonised because he acted strangely, wore funny clothes, lived in the desert and survived on locusts and honey. Now you think I can't be godly because I talk and eat with sinners and drink wine. Well, you'll find out that we're both from God! And that's going to blow your theology clean out of the water!"

Personally, I have no doubt that Jesus drank wine. We so need to take our eyes off the things that don't really matter and focus them on the things that really do. It seems that we try to make rules about our Christianity when the Word of God tells us that the letter of the law brings death, but the spirit of the law brings life (2 Corinthians 3:6). In so doing we push people away from the greatest relationship they can ever have. And guess who's job it is to change their hearts? That's right, it's His, not ours. How quickly we forget that when we see someone doing something we know isn't that godly. Suddenly we want to change them and heap condemnation on them instead of simply loving them back towards Jesus. Most of the issues we see in others are only symptoms growing on deeper issues. What we try to do is deal with the symptoms, not the issues. If you have greasy skin you will probably get spots. What I see is that you have spots and that you need to deal with the spots because you're spotty and people are put off by spotty people like you! Now you can't help that you have spots. You certainly didn't go out and buy a tin of spots and as it happens you're embarrassed by them too and would love to get rid of them, but nothing you do seems to help. And now that I have further embarrassed you by talking about them and telling you how awful and spotty you look, you don't want to talk to me any more or anyone in the church either. So you leave, hurt and still spotty! I don't blame you, so would I!

Some years ago some of our church's single people lived together in a big house full of bed-sits. Gradually, they began to talk to other people in the house about Jesus. They were interested and eventually one girl came to church and later gave her life to Jesus. Now it happened that she was living with her boyfriend, so two of the young people went to her and told her that she was "in sin" and should tell her boyfriend to leave. She didn't tell the boyfriend and he didn't leave the flat, but she left the church and never came back. Not only that, but the other non-Christians in the house heard about it and suddenly lost interest in hearing about Jesus and a potentially lovely outreach was shut down.

Years later, Janice and I spoke in a local fellowship and at the end of the teaching asked if anyone would like to give their life to Jesus. A few people responded and we were invited to pray for some of them later. One young lady caught our attention. Her heart had been truly gladdened by the redeeming wine of Jesus, strangely warmed and anything else you could think of! She didn't know whether to laugh or cry so she was doing both! She was drunk in the Spirit! Then she dropped her little bombshell question:

"I'm living with my boyfriend at the moment, should I go home and tell him to leave?"

I prayed one of those prayers that goes something like, "Help" and said to her, "Were you living with him when Jesus saved you?"

"Yes, of course," she replied,

"Then let's leave it up to Jesus to sort out the issue with you when He wants to."

You could see the sense of utter relief fill her as the tension of that issue drained away. I'm not sure some of the other leaders around me fully agreed, but bless them, they went along with me. Some months later we went back to the same church. There sat the young girl with her boyfriend and various parents, relatives and friends, many of them now saved. And the issues? Well Jesus was busy sorting them out in His time and His way and His order.

But having said all this, the central issue is not whether we think it right or wrong to drink wine, whether we think it wise or unwise, healthy or unhealthy. It is simply, as always, about whether or not we accept that God is talking to us about wine meaning wine, or wine meaning grape juice. The characteristics of both are very different and it is important we understand clearly what God would say to us when He talks about wine. Juice goes off, but wine is preserved. Jesus offers us wine to drink, not juice, because His blood will last forever, preserved by the heavenly alcohol, the presence of God in the heavenly tabernacle. A similar picture is given to us in the Bible when we see that the shewbread of Moses' tabernacle was still as fresh a week later as the day it was baked, even though it was left uncovered in a tent in the heat of the desert, because it stood exposed to the presence of God. God wants us to know that His blood is indestructible and eternal.

Chapter 12

Pests, Diseases and Problems

Like all plants, the vine is prone to a number of enemies. I wish with all my heart it were not so, but it is! Growing crops is not simply a matter of throwing a plant into a hole and coming back some months later to pick up the crop as any farmer or gardener will quickly tell you. Vines, as well as needing the vinedresser to constantly focus their attention on fruit production, are sensitive little plants that need lots of careful protection and tender loving care, as any good pastor will quickly tell you!

The Christian can learn simple lessons by looking at some of the primary enemies of the vine, though we need to remember that the final outcome of this vineyard is success, because,

"No weapon formed against you shall prosper."

(Isaiah 54:17)

As long as we understand that this word does not tell us we won't have to learn to fight the "weapon formed against us" we'll be alright. Christianity ensures each of us will have many battles to fight, but we are expected to learn how to overcome.

In 1863, a small aphid packed its bags, invited a few relatives to join him, and made the long transatlantic voyage to Europe. It liked the European vineyards so much it decided to stay and over the next few years, it slowly and inexorably wiped out almost all the vineyards of Europe. From there it continued its world trip reaching South Africa, Australia and New Zealand by the turn of the century. The bug bears the monstrous name *phylloxera vastatrix*, sometimes known as the grape louse, and its adventure in the nineteenth century was one of the worst agricultural disasters of history. Although it can affect all parts of the vine during the many stages of its life cycle, its most devastating attack is on the root system where it injects poisonous saliva as it cuts its way through the roots. The only real treatment against this pest is to graft a vine on to American rootstock, for they have developed immunity to the pest. All European vines are now grafted onto American rootstocks. The picture shows us the importance of making sure our roots are of the right type and properly established against our enemy. Jesus is, of course, the only root that will protect the Christian.

Recently, God has ministered a word of scripture to me with great power. Sometimes, I have questioned the Lord about my identity in Him. I am not talking here about the things that all of us are "in Christ". I mean the specific things God has called *me* to be. What is it He has specifically made me to be so that I can do the good works He has prepared beforehand for me to do? You might call it my personal destiny and calling; what makes me a uniquely different Christian from you and vice versa. One morning as I prayed, the Lord rebuked me sternly, telling me that whenever I allowed my foundational calling as a prophet to be undermined with doubt, I prevented Him from taking me further into my destiny. Now, I can no longer deny my calling in Him. I dare not, even when personal circumstances or experiences may shout to the contrary. My walk of faith includes the precious things He has spoken and given to me personally.

> *"If the foundations are destroyed,*
> *What can the righteous do?"*

(Psalm 11:3)

We should not be surprised by *phylloxera*, but forewarned. No wonder the vine spends so much time developing strong root systems. If my root system in God is poisoned, God can do nothing for me. If I constantly deny the cross and Christ crucified, my life in Him will die. If I constantly deny the calling He has on my life, my ministry will eventually die. I will not be attacked and cut off at my roots. Now, spiritual "phylloxera" cannot touch me, because my roots are secure in what Jesus calls me, for that is truly what I am.

Christians are too ready to accept a false humility that denies our calling, in preference to falling into pride that might spring up if we accept and acknowledge our specific job description in God. Both positions are a spiritual "phylloxera". How will we ever achieve what our Lord has in store for us if we continually allow ourselves to be cut off at our roots? It's high time we stood up and found enough grace to declare what we are in Christ. Honest recognition of our gifts and calling declares more about what we are not, than what we are, and simply allows us to become more focused and effective in what we do. Personally, I am proud of what my Lord has made me to be and I will give Him the glory for doing it. Like Paul, I am not ashamed of the gospel: it's a fantastic gift and my life is a testimony to its power to save men and transform lives.

There are three other major problems of attack for the vine. All three are fungal diseases. A fungus is a plant that lives by consuming other organic matter, like the mushroom, that consumes the fallen organic matter commonly found on the floor of the forest. But these diseases, though they function in the same way, are microscopic. Of the fungi that are attracted to the vine, *botrytis* produces a grey mould on young sappy cane, leaves, berries and bunch stems, rotting right through until the bunches drop to the ground; *oidium*, or powdery mildew, hardens the skin of the berries which then split open or just do not ripen; and *peronospera*, sometimes called downy mildew, attacks the leaves so that no sugars are produced to ripen or make fruit.

Christian beware. We really do have an enemy on the outside trying to prevent us from harvesting and we *will*, not we might, get attacked time and time again. The vine, like the Christian, is attacked in all areas of its growth. Roots, stem, leaves, bunch stems and berries. There really isn't anything else to try to disrupt in the "simple" vine. Unfortunately, the vine tells us we will face the same trouble – from baby Christian, through tender nurturing, preparation and training, to first signs of fruit and maturity. From our foundations onwards, we will face an enemy every time we respond to God and move towards a harvest. It becomes more obvious the further one goes through life. I am less surprised by attack now than in previous years. If we can get more used to it we will get more used to being "overcomers" and even on occasion, avoid it. Jesus taught us to pray that we be delivered from evil, which seems like the best sense of all.

Years ago, when our church was just starting in the house I lived in – the home of our senior leaders – we would meet on a Thursday evening. They were vibrant, powerful nights of enjoying God's presence in worship and the flow of His healing touch came as we ministered to one another. Some nights there were as many as seventy people crammed together in the house. But no matter how wonderful those Thursday evenings were, the daytime leading up to the evening was often quite the opposite. If we who lived there ever fell out, guess which day it was? If the washing machine ever broke down and overflowed, sickness struck, nasty letters from the bank arrived, or people fell out with us for not doing what they thought we should have done, guess what day it was? Of course, it was Thursday! Our enemy was trying to stop the fruit of the evenings happening. How many churchgoing couples, if we're honest, fall out trying to get to church on a Sunday morning? Things became so bad for us and so obvious that I made a cardboard sign and hung it over the stairs on Wednesday night, so that you literally bumped into it on your way downstairs on Thursday morning. It read, "WATCH OUT! TODAY IS THURSDAY!" It helped us remember and pretty soon we learned to pray for protection and overcome some of the problems.

When *botrytis* and mildew first hit my vineyard, I had lost the crop before I knew what the problem was. Now, I have a proper preventative spray programme in place so that the problems don't occur, and even if it does occur, I know how to deal with them quickly. I want that harvest. When a friend of mine began worship leading, all kinds of problems began to surface in her fifteen-year-old "happy" marriage. The enemy was contesting her call to move higher with her music ministry by attacking her close to home. Fortunately, both she and her husband soon realised what was happening, got some loving help to resolve the issues, and continued to press into God. They are mature Christians, overcomers who want a good harvest in their lives.

In many of the French vineyards, the growers plant roses at the head of the rows of vines. Although this looks quaint and adds a teasing splash of colour to the vineyards, they are nevertheless there for another purpose. Roses are susceptible to the same fungal diseases as the vines, yet show signs of the attack before it is visible on the vine. This gives the vinedresser time to react and spray the vines before the fungus can take hold. God in His mercy also gives us the chance to do something about problems by giving us people with the prophetic insight to forewarn the Church of impending issues that need resolution. We ignore the prophets and our leaders at our peril.

Vines also suffer from viruses, just as we do. The dictionary describes a virus as a "morbid poison" or "poison of a contagious disease (e.g. smallpox)" and even "moral poison". If fungi are external enemies, then viruses are internal enemies. All of us have them. Sometimes we catch them from other people, sometimes we carry them with us and never deal with them, but the effect of all of them is to prevent fruit from coming to harvest or even to bring death. There is really only one answer for an infected vine and that is to pull them up and burn them. The reality for the Christian who is infected with the poisons of warped or worldly mindsets, lifestyles or attitudes that contradict the life-giving statutes of God, is as stark as that for the vine. The only answer is death to self. Voluntary death allows the Holy Spirit to flow rivers of life-giving water through us for new life. Failure to offer this voluntary death will allow the poison to bring us involuntary death and block the works God wants harvest from in our lives.

It is a strange but true fact that my vines "bud burst" into life every year between 1st and 4th April. In eleven years this has been their pattern and generally it serves them well enough, but one year they got caught out by a late frost in mid May. Most of the new growth was "burnt" back by the frost and the vines had to start growth all over again. The net result was that, although they still produced grapes, they were so late in coming that they didn't have time to produce a good sugar content and thus needed a great deal of artificial sweetener to make up the difference. But it's just not the same as the natural sugar content and any wine you might try to make from it suffers greatly in depth and quality. Young Christians are very prone to getting burnt by attack in their early life in this way and it's up to those who understand these principles to cover them when their outlook looks frosty!

As if all these protagonists were not enough there is sadly one further way to lose a crop. The birds of the air hold a voracious appetite for grapes and can bring a heart-rending destruction to a vineyard in a very short space of time. Usually, they take the grapes before they are fully ripe. The only real answer is to cover the vines in the protection of a net. It is as if God allows the harvest to be taken before it can be offered. He allows the birds to consume it as a burnt offering is totally devoured by the fire. It's one thing to willingly give up a harvest for another's consumption, but quite a different matter to have it consumed without having the freedom to give it or be asked! When the Lord prematurely takes our harvest He is truly testing our hearts. How will we respond? By cursing God and giving up or by pressing into Him for restoration as Job did? Will we praise Him in all circumstances and also praise Him *for* all circumstances? Whatever the answers we need they are found only in Jesus, for by His stripes alone are we healed and as the great Vinedresser, He alone knows how best to treat our ills.

Chapter 13

The Process of Wine

Anyone who plants a vineyard does so for the harvest. Predominantly the vineyard is for wine. The Bible talks only of eating grapes four times and mentions raisins on only three occasions, but there are over one hundred and fifty references to wine.

Wine has so much to teach us. After the careful husbandry of the summer months, vineyards spring into bustling life for two short weeks as the harvest is gathered in. There is no waiting on the picked crop; it is taken straight to the crusher. I have a small crusher for my vineyard. It consists of two grooved and sharply angled wheels which revolve towards each other like a vicious barbed mangle. The grapes are fed from a hopper so that all of them pass between the rollers. The grapes are violently torn open and the juice begins to pour out. Only rarely does a grape escape the rollers and fall into the juice whole. It's a strange transformation. Grapes that have had a unique identity as part of a shapely and individual bunch, suddenly become completely anonymous to form a part of the wine. The skins, that for the summer gave individuality, will eventually be discarded. Wine production is more concerned with what's on the inside than the outside.

I often see this as a picture of the individual giving up their personal glory for the sake of the greater glory of the Church and by that, Jesus. If at this point the grapes represent people's lives, then the wine is surely a collective simile for the Church – a collection of sacrificial lives of the saints who have been crucified with Christ. There is great efficacy for the world in this that we should not lose sight of. Undoubtedly the wine of the Church is not in the same league as the wine, or the blood, of Jesus, but it is nonetheless vital to this dying world. It is the nature of costly sacrifice that makes it so precious. We know that the suffering of Jesus made Him unrecognisable as a human being, (His outer identity crushed like the grape), and separated Him from His Father, something He had never experienced before. He was called to die for the world, we are merely called to die to self, to have our self-life crushed out of us so we no longer live but Christ lives in us; and when the crushing is done, then comes pressing!

In the brutal middle ages some condemned people were pressed to death. Forced to lie on the ground, a board or door was placed over their body and stones and rocks gradually added until the unfortunate could breathe no more. The life was literally pressed out of them. The grape suffers this fate too, so that every drop of juice is released. When I press my crop, I screw the press until I can get no more juice, then release the screw and rough up the "cake" of pressed skins and repeat the process for a second time. Sometimes I am amazed to find an occasional whole grape amongst the skins – an escapologist from the crusher! In the Church we sometimes see such a person. Perhaps they have been around for years, never changing, whilst others around them have been transformed through the crusher and the press. They show an extraordinary resilience. But their time will come too. When God is turning the screw none escape!

The second and sometimes third pressing produces yet more juice. Where does it all come from? Precious juice lovingly stored within now pressurised to join with neighbours and adopt a new identity. Be encouraged to know that there is always more within than you think.

Wine makers call this juice the "must". It is cloudy and full of unwanted material, but it is sweet and rich in sugars – the more so the better for the resultant wine. Yeast is added to the must to start the fermentation process. Yeast is an organism which feeds on sugars and converts them to carbon dioxide and alcohol. As the process continues the yeast quickly multiplies and forms a thick layer of sediment in the must. Only a small amount of yeast is needed to start with and it soon affects the whole batch. Jesus referred to this action when He talked of the need to be aware of the false teaching of the Pharisees. But there are other yeasts which have a good and positive effect. The yeast of wine not only enhances the flavours of the wine but also protects it and preserves it. In the Church this should be mirrored by good, strong, balanced teaching coming from a healthy five-fold ministry, which will help us develop good character and find our true flavours, our destinies in Christ, and help preserve us when the going gets tough.

The yeast action continues until the available sugars have been consumed and converted. From that point on, the wine sits. It is worth noting that the business of producing the harvest is a job of work accomplished by the vine in cooperation with the vine-dresser. The vine has a natural ability to produce grapes, but to get the best results it needs a vinedresser to look after it. The business of making the wine requires only one thing of the vine: its complete willingness to give up its harvest to the hands of the winemaker. Sometimes you hear people marvel at how the Lord has used them or their lives to act as catalyst in some wonderful work of God, yet when you look into their lives you find men and women who are totally submitted to God and humble enough to be obedient to His still small voice, while He does the nurturing and drawing of others. He has a harvest wine He can work with.

Were I to make an indulgent observation here, I would tell of how this book has been so many years in the making and growing, and so many further months in the writing, all because I felt a compelling of the Lord to write it. That compelling required my cooperation to plant, observe, learn, collate and write, but having written, it is no longer in my hands. Having cooperated to harvest I must now relinquish control and allow Him to produce whatever wine He will from it. It is a very empty and exposed place to be in. Yet even if no one ever reads it, it has to be alright, because the greater joy has been cooperating with the master Vinedresser and getting to know Him better in the process. God once spoke to me through the picture of a potter's wheel. He told me that if I would allow Him to make me into a well-shaped wheel, I would spend hours with Him making pots that would serve in kings' palaces and the homes of the most noble. I, in the meantime, would remain in the potter's house, covered in the discomforting grime of wet clay, yet I would have the inestimable pleasure of working with the master Potter day in and day out. I'm learning it is better to be constantly with Him. Let Him elevate if He will or not, as long as we are with Him.

Making wine is a refining process of the winemaker's patience and experience. My several wise old Christian grey hairs have convinced me that God can be and is, much more patient than you or I! I do hope I am getting to the place where I can truly rest in the Lord's timing for those things He has placed on my heart. Winemakers call the act of pouring the wine off the sediment "racking" – a name which accurately evokes a sense of brutalisation one imagines must come upon a wine, quietly resting in the cool and dark, when it is so poured out. When the wine is quite still and clear it can be bottled, at which point its only requirement is that it "rest". It is, in our language, to be a human being not a human doing. It is to merely observe as the various flavours slowly combine together into a harmonious whole, knowing that it will not go off because of the preserving alcohol within it.

Once, my wife and I became involved in leading a ministry God had not called us to do. It was a learning experience I would not recommend having to go through and the ministry ended quite suddenly with pain and heartache and pressurised relationships. All the Lord would say to us was "stand". He sent seven people from outside the church just to tell us that. He even sent one man all the way from Scotland to Croydon just to tell us. Being obedient to that was one of the hardest things we have ever done. It lasted for about three years and you have no idea how many people came to us to ask if we would get involved with this, that or the other ministry, because, after all, we weren't "doing anything". Yet through the inactivity, our flavours began to come through. Instead of being a product of "what we did", we became more a product of "who we are" and our true ministry has come to the fore as God is teaching us to "rest" in Him.

This is surely true for us individually in the Church, but I do believe that if we accept wine as an epithet for the Church, or our churches, then there is a greater lesson of resting to learn. It is not that "doing" is wrong *per se*, more that when the time comes to be poured out, resting and maturing in Him will stand us in much better stead. Churches that learn the secrets of pressing into Him and seeing that as their highest priority, unhindered by Christian activity, are the ones that break new ground and see the power of God suddenly released.

There is a rest for the people of God, though it would seem at this time that many have not entered it. In any case, what does it mean when the Lord talks of entering that rest? Does it mean the Church is to do nothing and sleep all day? Of course not. The Bible says,

> "For he who has entered His rest has himself also ceased from his works as God did from His."
>
> (Hebrews 4:10)

People do not enter into God's rest because of disobedience or simply not obeying. (Those are two separate things by the way. It does not follow that you will be obedient if you are not disobedient!) Resting implies a ceasing from striving, just as the wine must remain still and at the mercy of the winemaker. When God placed Adam and Eve in the Garden of Eden, their job was to tend and look after it. I think they would have enjoyed doing so and in no way would it have been an irksome or laborious task. The Lord God had created a paradise on earth for them. Genesis 1:28 tells us that He had given them dominion, that is rule and authority, over the earth and all the creatures of the earth. It is safe to assume that they began to learn how to exercise some of that authority under God's loving guidance whilst they were in the garden. We know that this situation radically changed after they sinned and that the earth was cursed as a result. What was once a pleasure to join with God in doing now became painful toil. Where they had begun from a place of rest, they now had unrest.

> *"Cursed is the ground for your sake;*
> *In toil you shall eat of it*
> *All the days of your life."*
>
> (Genesis 3:17)

This unrest because of the curse of the ground was in the forefront of the minds of the Patriarchs. They would have known all too well the stories of the beauty and peace of the Garden of Eden told by Adam and Eve. But when Lamech had a child he saw something in his son of the works of God and prophesied over him through his name and in words. He called him Noah, which means rest, and prophesied,

> *"This one will comfort us concerning our work and the toil of our*
> *hands, because of the ground which the LORD has cursed."*
>
> (Genesis 5:29)

Now the curse on the ground was there because of man's sinful disobedience to God. What could possibly eradicate the effect of man's sin and restore him to his place of dominion over the earth? Well, from our position of history, we know there is only one thing that can do that, the blood of Jesus. Only the blood of Jesus restores us to our original Adamic relationship with God. We are at rest with Him only by the blood of the New Covenant of Jesus.

So when God told Noah to plant a vineyard, this was not an "off the cuff" command. It was a prophetic and beautifully set up request to highlight that *rest* would only return to us through the work He was starting again through Noah. Noah, if you like, would be the doorway through to the route by which God would complete His redemption of mankind. This redemption would only be complete through the blood of His Son and as His Son was to become the vine of God, Noah's restart would be prophetically accompanied by the planting of the vineyard of God. This prophetic importance is further strengthened by the fact that God then established the first covenant with man, placing His bow in the sky as a perpetual sign. This sign of relational restoration extends through the generations and God's further covenants to give us assurance of entering our rest with God. Noah is the righteous door through whom God began the process that would restore man to his original call in God. Our rest is dependent on our relationship with Him, just as Adam and Eve were dependent on their intimate relationship with Him in Eden. Lamech somehow saw this completed work in Noah and this enabled him to prophesy "rest" through Noah's name to the completed future work of Jesus.

Chapter 14

I Want My Vineyard Back

During my years as a Christian, I have occasionally heard preachers challenge congregations before they go on to talk about the end times. The gist of the challenge is to show that those who have been walking with the Lord for some years have observed a change in the spiritual "barometer" indicating the approach of the end times, showing that the spiritual temperature has increased considerably in the last couple of decades. A large majority of people witness to this.

A brief study of the relevant scriptures will soon show that this view should be supported to the extent that we may at times even feel like "the end is nigh!" Natural disasters are happening around the world with a frequency that makes it easy to become blasé about them. They can easily be to us "just another crisis" that will pass. Yet more wars rage over the surface of the earth than at any other time in history; there always seems to be a famine some-where or other, and morality has taken a nosedive. I remember listening to a taped prophetic vision received by David Wilkerson in the early eighties, talking about the end times. We were shocked by some of the things he talked about and simply could not "see" them happening, yet now, some twenty years or more further on, perhaps sixty-five percent of it would be considered "normal". Things have changed.

If we are as close to those days as many suspect, there should be some kind of parallel in the picture of God's vine – the Church – coming to the place of harvest. The two are linked in Scripture. In Revelation the angel is called to gather the harvest of the great vine of the earth at the end of the age. Just as Jesus is the vine and we are the grafted in branches, it is undoubtedly the New Testament Church's harvest that is being gathered at this end time.

So it is right that we ask the questions of the Church, "How near are we to harvest? Are we closer than ten or twenty years ago? Are we still being trained on the wires or are we busy making more wood than we need instead of channelling our energies into flowering and fruit?"

I suspect the answer is that as individual churches and nations we are in different stages of development, yet there is a general transition in process. The Church is changing and we must truly thank God it is.

The Church can in no way respond to God as it has done in the past and expect different results – the results we all long for so much. In Matthew 9:17, Jesus questioned such an idea as unthinkable, even to our limited knowledge and wisdom, when He referred to the stupidity of putting new wine into old wine-skins. Yet, despite even our own wisdom we still try to contain and control that which we cannot by our own regulation. God, it seems, would go even further than the obvious alternative – that new wine should go into flexible new wine skins – after all, they only go hard in time too. No, God says, "No container shall hold this new wine of My Spirit." He will be bound by no container, no inflexibility. His only boundary is boundless eternal love. The Church must somehow change to respond to that alone and for that alone will Christ claim His Bride. The only goal of our instruction in Christ is, *"love from a pure heart, from a good conscience, and from sincere faith"* (1 Timothy 1:5).

Perhaps ten or twenty years ago we were still flailing our arms about, wondering quite what was going on and making far too much wood; knowing salvation but not quite sure what it was supposed to mean while we are on this earth. By and large we were untrained, undisciplined and in control of our own destiny. John Wimber came to the UK in 1983 and delivered God's simple but profound message to His Church here: "I want my Church back." What a devastating word of rebuke, yet an encouraging word to change. How we have struggled since then as we have instantly responded in the affirmative and then squirmed and kicked and yelped and moaned every time He has clipped our branches and tied us down. We have sat through our winters unable to move. John Wimber again spoke to the Church in 1989 and asked an eight thousand strong conference, "Who feels as if their wheels have been taken off?" I loved the phrase because it was so descriptive of enforced immobility. So it seems did most of the delegates as they rose to acknowledge God's attention in their lives. God has been busy in His vineyard. He has been pruning and training and tying down. He earnestly desires His harvest.

We have been individual vines for years, but now we are vineyards with increasing definition and purpose. We are progressively understanding the need for intimacy and relationship with our Lord. Some can even rejoice in suffering, because they know it will produce a harvest of righteousness in their lives. Throughout villages, towns and cities, churches are realising that we are all part of the great vineyard of the earth that God has planted with His choice and noble vine, Jesus. Our individualism is becoming blurred for the sake of our Lord; progressively we want what He wants.

God is calling His Church to a higher place. Ultimately, I believe this is the place where we truly minister to Him as the consecrated and royal priesthood that we are. More than anything else God might want to say to His Church through the vine, I sense there is a deep desire in the heart of God for intimacy with His people. He calls Himself Emmanuel, "God with us", and is constantly talking about the intimacies of relationship. He wants to come in and dine with us; He wants us to separate ourselves to

Him; He wants us to be with Him just as Jesus sat at a table with John's head in His lap; He wants to dandle us on His knee like a proud Father and spend eternity with us. The vine and its relationship with the vinedresser is above all, a picture of the intimacy God wants with His children – the care He takes with each individual and the concern He has for the whole vineyard. But as yet, I do not sense this is a relationship the Church has generally grasped or welcomed. Many of us are still happily "doing church" the way we traditionally have. Our wineskins are tough but brittle and cannot cope with the volatile, gaseous fermenting wine God is making. It's dynamic and powerful stuff to change the world! We should not be surprised then, when our skins burst and we are left to watch what we thought was our wine, falling to the floor, wasted. God is shaking everything that's not nailed down in the Church at this time. We tend to change grudgingly if at all. Though if we learn, on the other hand, to embrace the changes God is bringing in, to welcome the guiding restrictions of the Lord, to love His discipline, knowing that it proves we are His children, and to cooperate with Him in producing harvest, things will turn out differently. We will, instead of distancing ourselves from Him, run to Him with arms outstretched, longing for His intimate touch and to talk with Him as He walks amongst the vines in the cool of the evening. We will grow to love intimate times with Him so much, that one day, He will call to us, His beloved, as His Bride. Intimacy is our inheritance with Him for all eternity. A time is coming when we will know Him in every single unveiled detail as He now knows us. No secrets, complete uncovered intimacy. This is the final battle for the Church. Will we run to Him?

It is imperative that we give up our own agendas for His; that we learn to put aside our petty differences and concentrate on our unity. I don't care if you have red hymnbooks and ours are green, have a classical style of worship or a rock and roll or jazz style. If you feel comfortable dressing up for church and I feel comfortable dressing down, does it really matter? As long as you believe the basic doctrine of 1 Corinthians 15:3–7 I can agree to walk with you. I may not agree with everything you do or believe, but I will do what I can to preserve peace between us and allow My Father to blend our flavours together into a wine that will slake the thirst of this weary world. And whatever else we may end up doing together, we don't need a theology to worship God in unity, and worship is a key to intimacy. I can sing songs of praise about my gorgeous wife all day long, but if she's in our bedroom in Croydon and I'm in a hotel in Glasgow or New York praising her, she won't get much of the benefit of my praise. She may hear about my singing and be blessed by the report of it, but what she really wants is for me to be with her in Croydon and tell her in person; when I come to her where she is and tell her how much I love her in her presence – that's worship and that's intimacy. That's coming towards her to kiss her and that's what our Lord is after.

Neither is intimacy a "nice to have" part of our faith, or an optional extra. The lesson of the vine is that without intimate cooperation with the vinedresser, the harvest will be sparse at best. Harvest improves the more we work with Him. It doesn't really matter what kind of grape we are or what kind of harvest we're expecting or looking for. If our main thrust is to "go and make disciples of all nations", or transform the world with great biblical teaching, or work amongst the homeless and disadvantaged, or excel at hospitality or administration or music or whatever else, our success will always bear relation to the level of intimacy with God we prioritise. Intimacy with God, knowing the Father, knowing Jesus, knowing the Holy Spirit, is what is supposed to fuel everything we do. Without intimacy with our Lord, we work in our own strength. With intimacy, He simply adds to us whatever we need.

It has taken me eleven years of trying to make wine to realise that the slightly sharp and bitter flavour that makes my wine undrinkable is caused by leaving the wine too long on the skins. That by which I define my uniqueness, my shape, my individuality, that I insist on holding onto as mine, is the very thing that prevents the rounded, smooth and true flavours of the wine developing, and more than that, actually taints it irrevocably. The wine is soured by me! God wants my individuality blended in the wine, but He doesn't want my ego. When we can get ourselves and our selfish motives and controlling behaviour out of the way for our Lord to truly reign over us; when all we want and pursue is intimacy with Him that in truth cries, "Yet not my will but Your will be done", when we reach out to each other without fear of betrayal, knowing that even if betrayal should come, we have a Great High Priest who comforts us in it because He has been there Himself and still overcomes . . . then we will see the Church emerge as the powerful wine that will intoxicate the world! We have no idea of the influence and power the Church has. It's the same power and authority to rule that God gave man in the Garden of Eden. A Christian friend of mine works with local government and was recently told by a councillor, "The Church is by far the most powerful force in local government, if only they would understand it, unite and use their influence." The world sees and understands the potential power of the Church; the Church often feels impotent and powerless and so would rather hold on to what little power we have in our local churches. Yet, not only do we have the authority of God, we also have the favour of God; it's what He wants.

In time God will create a new heaven and a new earth and He promises that there we will plant vineyards and eat their fruit, whilst He rejoices over what He has made (Isaiah 65:17–22). Then our rest will be eternal as foreigners will come and tend the vines and we will spend all our time tending our Lord as His priests, in His wonderful presence, being intimate with Him for eternity (Isaiah 61:5). Let us pray that we learn well the lessons of the vine and the vineyard the Lord has planted.

About the Author

Martin Richards trained and worked as a graphic artist before becoming a professional musician for ten years, working on cruise ships and in the West End of London in clubs and theatres. He had recently returned to the graphics industry when, in 1982, he was found by Jesus in a life-transforming conversion.

Martin was one of the founder members of Follys End Church, Croydon, UK, where he has been a leader since the beginning, serving the church in a variety of capacities. He came into full-time ministry in 2000 pursuing his gifting and calling as a prophet and an anointed prophetic worship musician and artist. For the last five years he and his wife Janice have run a School of Prophecy in Croydon and established "PIT Stop", a gathering for local area prophets. Martin also heads up 24/7 worship in Follys End and is a member of the Still Time Gospel Jazz Band, which travels extensively in the UK helping churches with their evangelistic efforts and leading worship.

Recently Martin has begun to travel in prophetic ministry, visiting such places as Finland, the Czech Republic, France and Spain. Janice is gifted in personal prophecy and has a unique welcoming ministry. Both have a passion to see creative arts-based ministries released in the Church.

Further copies of this book can be purchased online at:

www.webstore.follysend.org

We hope you enjoyed reading this New Wine book.
For details of other New Wine books
and a range of 2,000 titles from other
Word and Spirit publishers visit our website:
www.newwineministries.co.uk